It's Your Turn!

Round Robin Fun one block at a time!

WHAT ARE ROUND ROBIN QUILTS?

In a traditional round robin group, each participant or "owner" begins by making a center block for her quilt. The center blocks are passed in turn to each member who then adds a pieced or appliquéd "round", similar to adding a border. The completed quilt top is then sent back to the owner for quilting and finishing. Depending on the size of the project, the last few members to receive the quilt top could end up doing a lot of work to complete the larger rounds.

That's why I'm so excited to be able to introduce you to this fast and fun Block-by-Block, also known as Fill-In-the-Grid, variation of a round robin, which only requires you to make ONE block for each quilt in the group. When I first heard about this style of a round robin, I knew it had to be wonderful! In our busy lives we don't always have time to take part in a traditional round robin, but most of us can find time to make one block each month. After hosting and participating in a Block-by-Block round robin, I was hooked and I know you will be too!

Happy Quilting!
— Pat

THE FUN BEGINS

Start with a common denominator, a talented, dynamic quilt designer/teacher, Pat Sloan, who likes to have fun and enjoys experimenting with new techniques. Add four strangers who share a love of quilting and what do you get? The makings of a round robin quilt group! The members of this group include Margi, Pat's good friend who helps with her Internet quilting groups; Roseann, a talented quilt shop owner; Sandee, an associate editor for McCall's Quilting; and Jean, a quilt technical writer for Leisure Arts.

Using this group's experiences as her examples, Pat shares with you her tried and true guidelines for organizing, hosting, and participating in her favorite version of a round robin quilt group. Pat also provides step-by-step instructions for making each participant's quilt, excerpts from their journals, and some of their favorite recipes! Read on as Pat reveals the details of this fun quilt-making concept.

WHY JOIN A ROUND ROBIN GROUP?

1. Learn new design skills - Round robins will stretch your design abilities, and bring out skills you didn't know you had. For example, Jean's nautical quilt gave me a reason to research and create a great lighthouse for her quilt!

2. Expand your color palette - We often tend to overuse comfortable and familiar color combinations. Roseann actually had to get some bright purple for Margi's quilt, since she didn't even own any!

3. Make new friends - Whether you join an online group (as we did) or a local group, chances are that you will not know everyone. By the end of the project, you'll have a whole new group of quilting buddies!

4. Employ new techniques - Do you have a ruler that needs testing? Want to learn how to use a bias binding maker? Sandee had the chance to try some new embellishing techniques when she used beads, buttons, and trimmings on her blocks!

Have you been asked to be in a round robin but never took the plunge? There is so much to be gained from being in a round robin group.

Here are my "Top 10" reasons to join:

5. Experiment with fabrics - Several of us used wool on our blocks and included extra pieces in our packages. Margi, who had wanted to try working with wool, had fun experimenting with an unfamiliar fiber.

6. Work outside your norm - Maybe you've only made pieced quilts or you're stuck on appliqué. In our group, Jean, who usually makes symmetrical quilts, had the chance to try asymmetrical designs — a style which she now loves!

7. Keep Motivated - When you quilt for yourself you often don't have to meet a deadline. Most Block-By-Block round robins are set up for a short turn-around time. You can't put these projects away for months and not work on them!

8. Learn to trust your instincts - We often agonize over which fabric to use in a quilt. We test fabrics, show all our friends, go shopping for more fabric...sound familiar? Just go with your instincts. I find that people who stick with their first choice usually make good decisions.

9. Work as a Team - You will be part of a group of friends who are willing to chat, share, bounce ideas off each other, and help if you have a creative or technical problem!

10. To have fun - The best reason of all to join a round robin is to have fun — lots and lots of fun!

GETTING ORGANIZED

WELCOME LETTER

Although you will work as a team and make a lot of group decisions, every Block-By-Block round robin needs someone to act as organizer/host, as I have for the Block-By-Block round robin featured in this book. This person is responsible for setting up the schedule, rules, guidelines, and is the main point of contact when questions arise.

To help you plan your Block-By-Block round robin, pages 4-8 contain a copy of my Welcome Letter, Overview, Sample Group List, Sample Mailing Schedule, Rules, and Guidelines. Also included are some tips and suggestions for adapting the Rules and Guidelines to any Block-By-Block round robin group.

Tip: I find if I work on a project as soon as it comes in, I can usually turn it around in a few days.

Hi Margi, Sandee, Jean, and Roseann!

I'm so happy you can play with me to make this book a possibility!

In the attached Overview, Mailing Schedule, Rules, and Guidelines, I've outlined everything I think we need to know. After reading them, please let me know if something doesn't make sense or you need clarification!

I do have a few questions that I'd like you to respond to as soon as you can:
1. Is all your mailing information correct?

2. Will the schedule work for you? It is not quite evenly spaced because of some holiday and travel issues. I'm giving us a breather for the start date, and then we need to hustle through.

3. Do you want to do hand work or machine work? I'm in favor of fusible appliqué and machine blanket stitch to save time. Let me know if that is an issue for you.

4. And the last item is your theme. Will each of you tell me your theme in the next week? Then I can be sure we are not duplicating themes and that we have variety. You don't have to decide what your starter block will look like, just the theme.

I'd love for one quilt to use bright fabrics if any of you feel comfortable with that.

I'd also like for us to share photos of the quilts in progress. To make it simple we can just send them in emails to each other. If you have any suggestions for other ways to display the photos, let me know.

Margi and I have both participated in this type of group. She has been a moderator on my Block-By-Block round robin Internet groups and can also answer questions about how the process works.

My goal is for us to enjoy being in the group, have fun making quilts, stretch our design abilities, and for each of you to make new friends!

Hugs,
Pat

OVERVIEW

To begin, *each* member/owner creates a fabric grid to be used as a "design board" and a starter block that reflects a theme.

The grids and blocks are mailed, in turn, to each member who then makes a block. To obtain the goal of having the grids completely filled by the time the quilts return to the owners, each person can add one or more blocks.

The process continues until all group members have added a block(s) to each grid. The completed grids, with blocks attached, are returned to the owners for assembly and finishing.

Each owner now has a wonderful friendship quilt and lots of memories to cherish!

SAMPLE GROUP LIST

	NAME	E-MAIL	ADDRESS	PHONE
1	Margi			
2	Pat			
3	Jean			
4	Sandee			
5	Roseann			

SAMPLE MAILING SCHEDULE

October 8	Owners begin work on Grid and Starter Blocks
November 29	Grid and Starter Block completed and mailed
December 31	Round 2 completed and mailed
January 24	Round 3 completed and mailed
February 21	Round 4 completed and mailed
March 31	Round 5 completed and mailed back to owner
April 31	Quilts completed

OUR RULES

The grids

1. The grids serve as temporary design boards for block placement.

2. The group *or* the organizer determines grid size. I suggest making wall hangings using a 24" x 32" grid. Muslin or a similar fabric works well for the grid fabric.

3. Cut the grid fabric at least 1" larger on all sides than the desired grid size. Leaving at least 1" on each outside edge, draw a grid of 4" x 4" squares on the muslin. Our grids will be 6 squares across by 8 squares high (**Fig. 1**).

Tip: You can zigzag or hem the edges of your grid to keep the edges from unraveling.

Tip: If your group has more than 5 members, you may choose to use more grid squares to make a larger finished grid.

Fig. 1

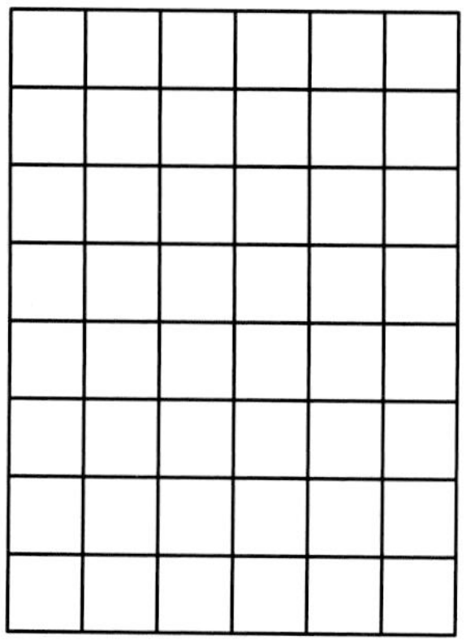

The blocks

1. Only use 100% quilters' quality cotton, unless using a specialty fabric such as wool.

2. Wash your fabrics or test for colorfastness.

3. Please strive for accurate $^1/_4$" seams.

4. Blocks can be pieced, appliquéd, or a combination of the two.

5. Techniques to be used, such as fusible or hand appliqué, will be decided by the group.

Tip: You might want to have a mixture of techniques so each person in the group can use the one they like the best.

6. For our grids, I recommend the starter block(s) be 12" square or a rectangle of a similar size. Refer to **Figs. 2- 5** for some suggested **finished** starter block sizes and grid placement.

Tip: For larger groups or when working on a larger grid, you may need to adjust the size of your starter blocks.

Fig. 2

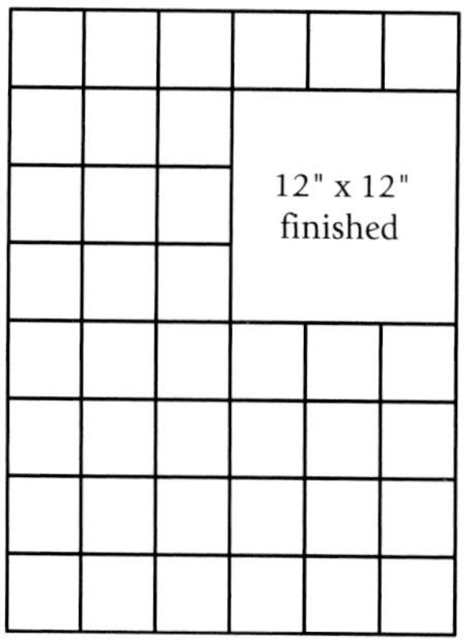

12" x 12" finished

Fig. 3

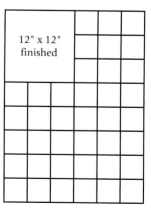

12" x 12" finished

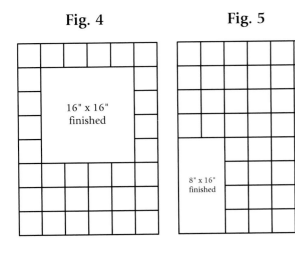

Fig. 4

16" x 16" finished

Fig. 5

8" x 16" finished

Miscellaneous

1. The group decides if they want to show the quilts in progress. For this Block-By-Block round robin, we will share photos after each round.

Tip: For my Internet group we have folders for photographs so the owner can elect to peek or not.

2. When planning or working on a block, you may consult with any participant other than the owner.

3. Unless the owner includes specifics in her package (for example; no orange fabrics), there are no set rules as to what can be added to a block.

4. You must be committed to completing the project.

5. The Golden Rule is to work on another person's project as you would have them work on yours.

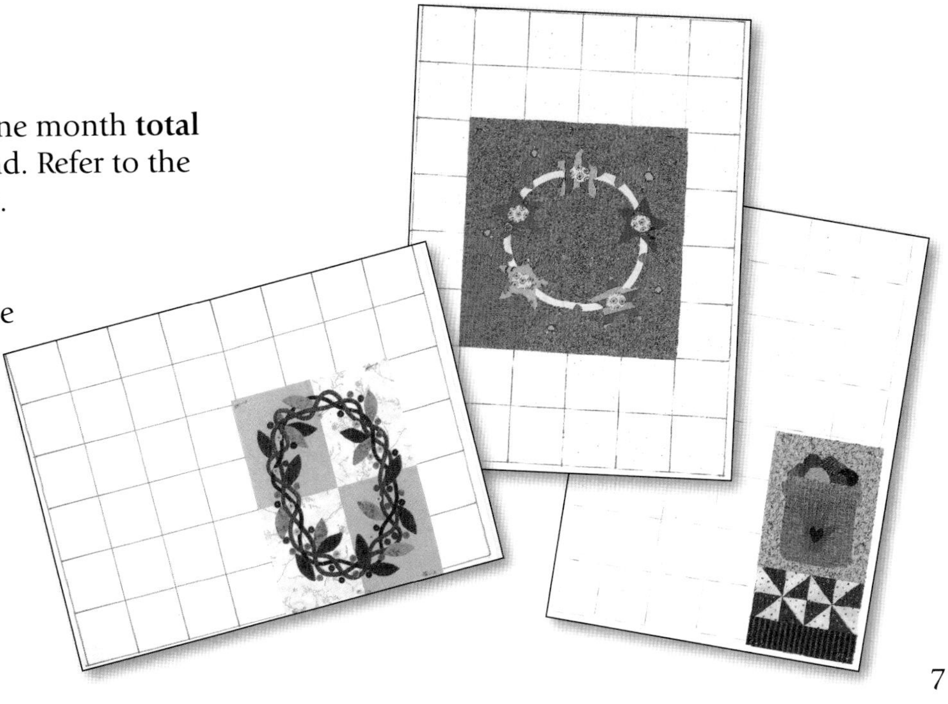

7. After the starter block is placed, the remaining members will divide, as equally as possible, the remaining grid squares in order to fill the whole grid with their blocks.

8. When your block is finished, write your name directly onto the grid squares that it covers and then pin or hand baste your addition to the grid. This will help the owner with placement when she is assembling the quilt top.

Mailing

1. You have a maximum of one month **total** to complete and mail each round. Refer to the mailing schedule for exact dates.

2. Each member mails to the next member on the list. For example, member 1 always mails to member 2, member 2 to member 3, etc., and the last member always mails to member 1.

OUR GUIDELINES

In addition to the Rules, you may wish to establish Guidelines, as we did. They are not necessary to complete a Block-By-Block round robin, but can make it more personal and fun.

1. Each of us will either hand-make or purchase a journal, which will be included in our mailing packages. On the first few pages record your ideas and inspirations, explain your quilt's theme, and note any special requests you have. Each group member will fill in a page or two of your journal about their addition to your grid.

2. Include in your package any fabric or trims that you think the other members might like to use. You could also add any photos for inspiration or other items that might help the group create your quilt.

3. Each of us will make a label of our own choosing. Include your label in your package so all the members can sign it.

4. Friends, Food, and Quilting just seem to go together! Since we quilters love *collecting* recipes, why don't we each include one in our journals? I have very few recipes since my family doesn't cook — ha ha! But I do have a couple.

5. I'm going to add some words or phrases to some of the blocks I make; feel free to do the same.

6. I would LOVE all the quilts to have a very different "look." In my Internet group, we had a quilt that used all blue fabrics for the block backgrounds, which was totally awesome! Also, there was a good mix of pastel and bright quilts.

7. We will email each other as a group to keep track of where we are, show photos, ask questions, etc.

8. When your grid returns, you may find that some blocks are not quite the correct size. Feel free to trim down or add to a block to make it "fit." Now is the time to add borders, sashings, or whatever you choose to finish the piece and make it your "own."

When the responses to my welcome letter came in, a few minor changes to addresses were noted, the schedule was approved, hand appliqué was chosen as the preferred stitching method, themes had been selected, and our gvidlines were established. Our group was ready and eager to begin!

Yardage is based on 43"/44" (109 cm/112 cm) wide fabric with a "usable" width of 40" (102 cm) after trimming selvages and shrinkage.

...o cut fabric.
...allowances.
...te Cutting,
...plates from
...mmediately
...nstructions.

..., page 115,
...ps. Refer to
...r appliqué
...mbroidery.

JO-ANN FABRICS AND CRAFTS
1161 COMMERCIAL ST.
ASTORIA, OREGON
503-325-3377

N   8694119 IT'S YOUR TURN!
   1   @   24.95   24.95
      40% OFF CURRENT   -9.98
           SUB-TOTAL   14.97
              TOTAL   14.97
                  00544B AUTH
CC# XXXXXXXXXXXX0422

              VISA   14.97

STORE #:1726 - 0001   ASSOCIATE #:333
07/20/07   TRANS #: 004617   11:03 AM

       THANKS, COME AGAIN!
             ALAN

       THANK YOU FOR
     SHOPPING WITH US
          TODAY

BEFORE YOU START YOUR PROJECT

Dear Sandee, Roseann, Margi, and Jean,

For me, the magic of Christmas starts with stockings. They hang from mantels, doorknobs, chairs, and banisters. They can be fun or elegant and are sometimes silly. As a little girl, I wondered what Santa would put in my stocking. And of course, the stocking was the first thing I opened on Christmas morning. What represents the magic of Christmas to you? I can't wait to see what you add to my quilt; it will be a treasure for years to come. I've enclosed some of the candy cane fabric for you to use. The recipe I've included is wonderful — it comes from my husband's grandmother and I've made it many times.

Thank you for playing the "Grid Game" Round Robin with me!

Pat

MAGIC *of* CHRISTMAS

Owner: **Pat Sloan**
Machine quilted by: **Cathy Leitner**

Finished Quilt Size: 36" x 47" (91 cm x 119 cm)

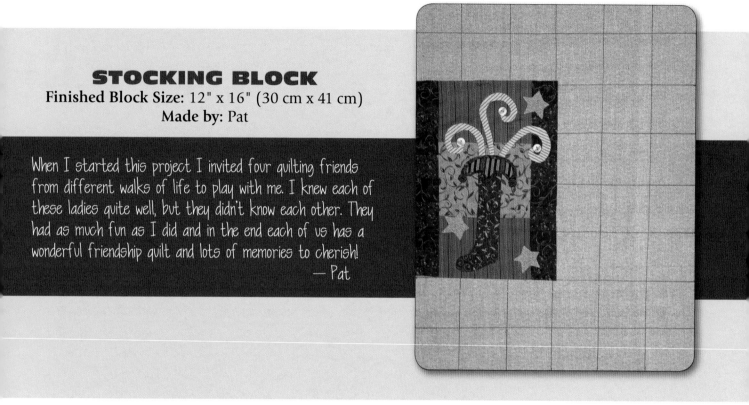

STOCKING BLOCK

Finished Block Size: 12" x 16" (30 cm x 41 cm)
Made by: Pat

When I started this project I invited four quilting friends from different walks of life to play with me. I knew each of these ladies quite well, but they didn't know each other. They had as much fun as I did and in the end each of us has a wonderful friendship quilt and lots of memories to cherish!

— Pat

Yardage Requirements

One 8$^1/_2$" x 5$^1/_2$" (22 cm x 14 cm) rectangle **each** of 2 gold print fabrics (background)
One 8$^1/_2$" x 6$^1/_2$" (22 cm x 17 cm) rectangle of gold print fabric (background)
One 2$^1/_2$" x 18$^1/_2$" (6 cm x 47 cm) strip **each** of 1 red and 1 green print fabric (Strip Set)
Assorted scrap fabrics (appliqués)
You will also need:
Template plastic
Assorted sizes and colors of buttons

Cutting Out The Pieces

From assorted scrap fabrics:
- Cut 2 candy canes (**A**). Cut 1 candy cane reversed (**Ar**).
- Cut 1 stocking (**B**).
- Cut 1 stocking cuff (**C**).
- Cut 1 stocking cuff trim (**D**).
- Cut 1 stocking toe (**E**).
- Cut 1 stocking heel (**F**).
- Cut 3 stars (**G**).

Assembling The Block

1. Sew background rectangles together to make **block background**.
2. Sew red and green print strips together to make **Strip Set**. Cut across Strip Set at 2$^1/_2$" intervals to make 8 **Unit 1's**.

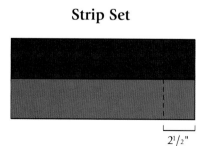

Strip Set   Unit 1 (make 8)

2$^1/_2$"

8. Sew 4 Unit 1's together to make 1 **block side border**. Make 2 block side borders. Sew 1 border to each side of block background.

Block Side Border (make 2)

4. Work in alphabetical order to **Needle-Turn Appliqué** pieces **A - G** to block background.
5. Sew buttons on candy canes and stocking cuff to complete **Stocking Block**.

Stocking Block

Finished Block Size: 12" x 12" (30 cm x 30 cm)
Made by: Jean

Hi Pat!

Growing up in the South, Christmas Day was likely to be spent in short sleeves, riding bikes, or walking on the beach. But, oh, how I wished for snow! I would watch Christmas movies and could only dream about how wonderful it must be to build a snowman, go ice-skating, or ride on a sled.

This year, I received an early magical Christmas present when it snowed on December 22nd. What fun it was to be curled up in my favorite chair, appliqueing a snowman block while outside my window the world was covered in white and a jolly snowman stood watch!

Jean

Yardage Requirements

One 12½" x 12½" (32 cm x 32 cm) square of navy print fabric (background)

One 4½" x 12½" (11 cm x 32 cm) rectangle of white print fabric for snow (**H**)

7" x 10" (18 cm x 25 cm) rectangle of white wool felt for snowman (**R**)

Assorted scrap fabrics (appliqués)

You will also need:

Template plastic

Black and orange embroidery floss

Red and white No. 3 pearl cotton

Small black buttons

Cutting Out The Pieces

Before cutting out snowman, give your wool felt a fluffier look by hand washing vigorously in hot water and tumbling dry. **Note:** *When cutting out snowman (R), do not add seam allowances.*

From assorted scrap fabrics:

- Cut 2 tree trunks (**I**).
- Cut 1 of each tree (**J-L**).
- Cut 1 hat (**M**).
- Cut 1 hatband (**N**).
- Cut 1 scarf (**O**).
- Cut 1 of each scarf end (**P** and **Q**).

From white wool felt:

- Cut 1 snowman (**R**).

Assembling The Block

Use 2 strands of floss for all embroidery.

1. Trim top edge of white print rectangle (**H**) to make a gentle curve.
2. With right sides facing up and bottom edges even, place white print rectangle (**H**) on top of background square. **Needle-Turn Appliqué** top curved edge of white print rectangle to background square to make **block background**.
3. Work in alphabetical order to **Needle-Turn Appliqué** pieces **I - Q** to block background.
4. Use white pearl cotton to **Blanket Stitch** snowman (**R**) to block background.
5. Use orange floss to **Satin Stitch** a nose and black floss to **Stem Stitch** a mouth on snowman.

6. To make pompom, cut a strip of cardboard 1" wide. Wind red pearl cotton around cardboard until it is ¼" thick in the middle or approximately 40 wraps (**Fig. 1**). Carefully slip wrapped pearl cotton off cardboard and firmly tie a seperate length of pearl cotton around the middle; leave ends long enough to attach pompom to hat (**Fig. 2**). Cut loops on both ends and trim pompom into a smooth ball; hand stitch to top of hat.

Fig. 1

Fig. 2

7. Sew 2 buttons on face for eyes and 3 buttons on body to complete **Snowman Block**.

Snowman Block

DEAR SANTA BLOCK

Finished Block Size: 12" x 12" (30 cm x 30 cm)
Made by: Sandee

Dear Pat,

The mystery of Christmas to me was SANTA! When I was little, my aunt and grandmother would come over and we would bake and decorate all kinds of Christmas cookies. On Christmas Eve, I would select some cookies (usually my favorites) and fix a plate, pour a big glass of milk, and place them on the table along with my note to Santa.

We would go to Christmas Eve church services and Santa would visit. I always wondered how that sled, filled with toys and Santa (after he ate all those cookies), ever got off the ground!

Sandee

Yardage Requirements

One $9^{1}/_{2}$" x $5^{1}/_{2}$" (24 cm x 14 cm) rectangle of pink striped fabric (background)
One $9^{1}/_{2}$" x $4^{1}/_{2}$" (24 cm x 11 cm) rectangle of red print fabric (background)
$^{1}/_{8}$ yd (11 cm) of gold print fabric (borders)
Assorted scrap fabrics (appliqués)

You will also need:
Template plastic
Black and green embroidery floss
Assorted sizes and colors of buttons and beads
6" (15 cm) of white baby rickrack
Air-soluble fabric marking pen

Cutting Out The Pieces

From gold print fabric:
- Cut 2 side borders 2" x $9^{1}/_{2}$" and 2 top/bottom borders 2" x $12^{1}/_{2}$".

From assorted scrap fabrics:
- Cut 1 milk (**S**).
- Cut 1 glass base (**T**).
- Cut 1 letter (**U**).
- Cut 1 plate (**V**).
- Cut 2 star cookies (**W**).
- Cut 3 round cookies (**X**).
- Cut 3 leaves (**Y**).
- Cut 1 gingerbread man (**Z**).

Assembling The Block

Use 2 strands of floss for all embroidery.

1. Sew background rectangles together to make **block background.**
2. Sew side and then top/bottom borders to block background.
3. Using a light box or sunny window and air-soluble fabric pen, trace words onto piece **U**. Use black floss to **Backstitch** over traced words.
4. Work in alphabetical order to **Needle-Turn Appliqué** pieces **S - Y** to block background.
5. Cut rickrack into 4 equal lengths. With raw ends of rickrack extending beyond edges of appliqué, sew rickrack to arms and legs of gingerbread man (**Z**). Trim rickrack even with raw edges of appliqué. **Needle-Turn Appliqué** gingerbread man to block background.
6. Use black floss to **Stem Stitch** the outline of a glass around milk appliqué and to make a **Back Stitch** mouth on gingerbread man.
7. Use green floss to **Stem Stitch** a vein through the center of each holly leaf.
8. Sew beads or buttons to the center of each cookie, on gingerbread man for eyes and on body, and on each holly leaf to complete **Dear Santa Block.**

Dear Santa Block

Finished Block Size: 12" x 8" (30 cm x 20 cm)
Made by: Roseann

Hi Pat,

I came from one of those families that raised the roof at Christmas with all the talking and laughter. There were seven kids in our family and we had 55 first cousins on the Waldoch side. At Thanksgiving, all the cousins' names were put in a hat and drawn out while the aunts recorded who had each name for a Christmas present. Everyone took turns hosting Christmas and nobody missed coming. I chose my theme because the only time I wasn't home for the holidays was when I was in the Army. I was stationed in Virginia and couldn't take leave. My heart broke from not being home with my family. When I see the movie "All Hearts Come Home for Christmas", it has a special meaning to me.

Roseann

Yardage Requirements

One 7" x 5½" (18 cm x 14 cm) rectangle
of navy print fabric (background)
One 7" x 3½" (18 cm x 9 cm) rectangle
of white print fabric (background)
One 3½" x 8½" (9 cm x 22 cm) rectangle
of red print fabric (background)
One 3" x 8½" (8 cm x 22 cm) rectangle
of pink striped fabric (background)
Assorted scrap fabrics (appliqués)
Assorted scraps of wool (tree, heart, and stars)

You will also need:

Template plastic
Black, tan, gold, red, grey, and green
embroidery floss
Assorted sizes and colors of buttons and beads
Air-soluble fabric marking pen

Cutting Out The Pieces

Note: When cutting out appliqué pieces AA – JJ, do not add seam allowances.

From assorted scrap fabrics:

- Cut 1 house side (**AA**).
- Cut 1 house front (**BB**).
- Cut 1 roof (**CC**).
- Cut 1 chimney (**DD**).
- Cut 1 door (**EE**).
- Cut 1 window (**FF**).

From scraps of wool:

- Cut 1 tree (**GG**).
- Cut 1 heart (**HH**).
- Cut 2 stars (**II**).
- Cut 1 star (**JJ**).

Assembling The Block

Use 2 strands of floss for all embroidery unless otherwise noted.

1. Sew navy and white background rectangles together to make **Unit 1**. Sew red background rectangle to left side and pink striped background rectangle to right side of Unit 1 to make **block background**.

2. Using a light box or sunny window and air-soluble fabric pen, trace words onto block background. Use black floss to **Backstitch** over traced words.

3. Use tan floss to **Blanket Stitch** appliqué pieces **AA**, **BB**, **DD**, and **FF** and black floss to **Blanket Stitch** pieces **CC** and **EE** to block background.

4. Use grey floss to **Backstitch** smoke curls coming out of chimney.

5. Use green floss to **Straight Stitch** a wreath on door and a vine across heart. Use 1 strand of green floss to **Straight Stitch** piece **GG** to block background.

6. Use 1 strand of gold floss to **Straight Stitch** pieces **II** and **JJ** and 1 strand of red floss to **Straight Stitch** piece **HH** to block background.

7. Sew buttons on tree. Sew beads on wreath and vine to complete **Home For Christmas Block**.

Home For Christmas Block

When my grid came home, I added
sashing strips between some of the
blocks, similar to the one Margi used
on the bottom of her Sugar Plum Fairies
Block. Then, Margi and I ended up using
the same fabric (in different colors) for
our borders! Are we friends or what?
— Pat

17

SUGAR PLUM FAIRY BLOCK

Finished Block Size: 8" x 25" (20 cm x 64 cm)
Made by: Margi

Pat,

The mystical nature of Christmas captivated me from the earliest time I can remember. Whimsical figures like sugarplum fairies and elves added to the excitement of the holidays. Christmas has always been a favorite time because my family has always wrapped the holiday in tradition and put children at the center of the celebration. To this day, I still believe in Santa and what he represents to my wonderful, loving family. I am so blessed!

Margi

Yardage Requirements

One 7" x 6½" (18 cm x 17 cm) rectangle **each** of 3 gold print fabrics (backgrounds)
Three 1½" x 8" (4 cm x 20 cm) strips **each** of 1 red and 1 green print fabric (Strip Set)
⅛ yd (11 cm) of red print fabric (borders)
Assorted scrap fabrics (appliqués)

You will also need:
Template plastic

Cutting Out The Pieces
From red print fabric:
- Cut **2** top/bottom borders 1½" x 24" and 2 side borders 1¼" x 8½".

From assorted scrap fabrics:
- Cut 1 of each wing (**KK - MM**).
- Cut 6 feet (**NN**).
- Cut 3 dresses (**OO**).
- Cut 3 dress trims (**PP**).
- Cut 3 faces (**QQ**).
- Cut 3 hair shapes (**RR**).

Assembling The Block
1. Working in alphabetical order and using pieces **KK – RR**, arrange and then **Needle-Turn Appliqué** 1 Sugar Plum Fairy to each background rectangle.

2. Alternating colors, sew strips together to make **Strip Set**. Cut across Strip Set at $1^1/2$" intervals to make 4 **Unit 1's**.

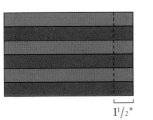

Strip Set **Unit 1** (make 4)

$1^1/2$"

3. Sew 4 Unit 1's and 3 Sugar Plum Fairies background rectangles together to make **block background**.
4. Sew top/bottom and then side borders to block background to complete **Sugar Plum Fairies Block**.

Sugar Plum Fairies Block

MAKING THE QUILT TOP

Sashings and Borders

Yardage Requirements

$1/4$ yd (23 cm) of green print fabric (sashings)
$1/8$ yd (11 cm) of red print fabric (sashings)
$1/4$ yd (23 cm) of gold print fabric #1 (inner border)
$1/4$ yd (23 cm) of gold print fabric #2 (words)
1 yd (91 cm) of navy blue print fabric (outer border and binding)
$3^1/8$ yds (2.9 m) of backing fabric

You will also need:
Template plastic
44" x 55" (112 cm x 137 cm) rectangle of batting

Cutting Out The Pieces

From green print fabric:
- Cut 1 bottom sashing strip $1^1/2$" x $24^1/2$".
- Cut 1 side sashing strip $1^1/2$" x $27^1/2$".
- Cut 1 top sashing strip $1^1/2$" x $25^1/2$".
- Cut 3 sashing squares $2^1/2$" x $2^1/2$".
- Cut 1 sashing rectangle $2^1/2$" x $8^1/2$".

From red print fabric:
- Cut 5 sashing squares $2^1/2$" x $2^1/2$".

From gold print fabric #1:
- Cut 2 inner top/bottom borders $1^1/2$" x $27^1/2$".
- Cut 2 inner side borders $1^1/2$" x $36^1/2$".

From gold print fabric #2:
- Cut 1 of each letter **THE MAGIC**.

From navy print fabric:
- Cut 2 outer top/bottom borders $4^1/2$" x $35^1/2$".
- Cut 2 outer side borders $4^1/2$" x $38^1/2$".
- Cut 5 binding strips $2^1/4$" wide.

Assembling The Quilt Top Center

*Refer to **Quilt Top Diagram**, page 20, for placement.*

1. Sew 2 red print sashing squares and green print sashing rectangle together to make **sashing strip #1**; sew to bottom edge of Stocking Block.

Sashing Strip #1 (make 1)

2. Sew 3 red and 3 green print sashing squares together to make **sashing strip #2**; sew to bottom edge of Dear Santa Block.

Sashing Strip #2 (make 1)

3. Sew Stocking and Home For Christmas Blocks together to make **Unit 1**.
4. Sew Dear Santa and Snowman Blocks together to make **Unit 2**.
5. Sew Units 1 and 2 together to make **Unit 3**.
6. Sew bottom sashing strip to bottom edge of Unit 3.
7. Sew side sashing strip to right side of Unit 3.
8. Sew top sashing strip to top edge of Unit 3.
9. Sew Unit 3 and Sugar Plum Fairies Block together to make **Quilt Top Center**.

Adding The Borders

1. Matching centers and corners, sew side then top/bottom inner borders to quilt top center.
2. Repeat Step 1 to sew outer borders to quilt top center.
3. **Needle-Turn Appliqué** the words, THE MAGIC, on bottom border to complete **Quilt Top**.

COMPLETING THE QUILT

1. Follow **Quilting**, page 117, to mark, layer, and quilt as desired. Our quilt is machine quilted with stars, loops, and holly leaves in the block backgrounds and outer border. There is outline quilting around each appliqué.
2. Follow **Making Straight-Grain Binding** and **Pat's Machine-Sewn Binding**, page 121, to bind quilt using **binding strips**.

Quilt Top Diagram

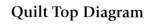

Pat's Apple Cake
- 3 cups flour
- 2 cups sugar plus 5 tablespoons sugar
- 1 cup vegetable oil
- 3 apples
- 4 eggs
- 1/4 cup orange-pineapple juice
- 2 1/2 teaspoons baking powder
- 1 teaspoon salt
- 2 teaspoons cinnamon
- 1/2 cup chopped nuts

Pre-heat oven to 350°

Grease and flour a bundt cake pan.
Peel and core apples. Chop into small chunks; set aside.
Mix 5 tablespoons sugar and cinnamon; set aside.
Beat remaining ingredients together.
Pour 1/2 the batter into pan.
Arrange 1/2 the apples on top of batter; sprinkle with 1/2 cinnamon sugar.
Pour remaining batter into pan.
Top with remaining apples and cinnamon sugar.
Bake 60 minutes... TEST... EAT!

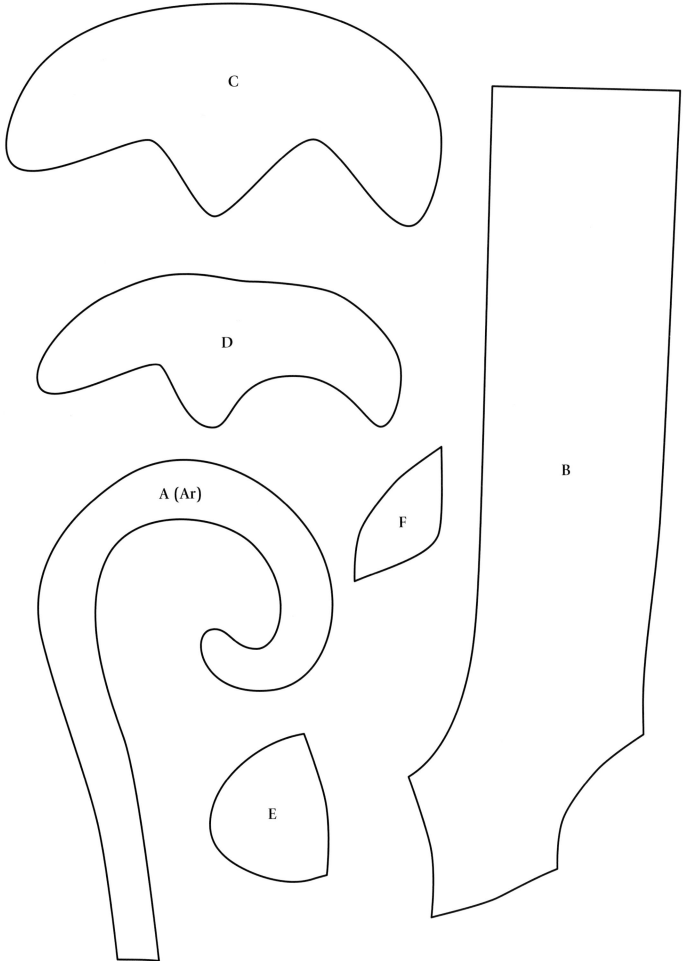

J

R

I

G

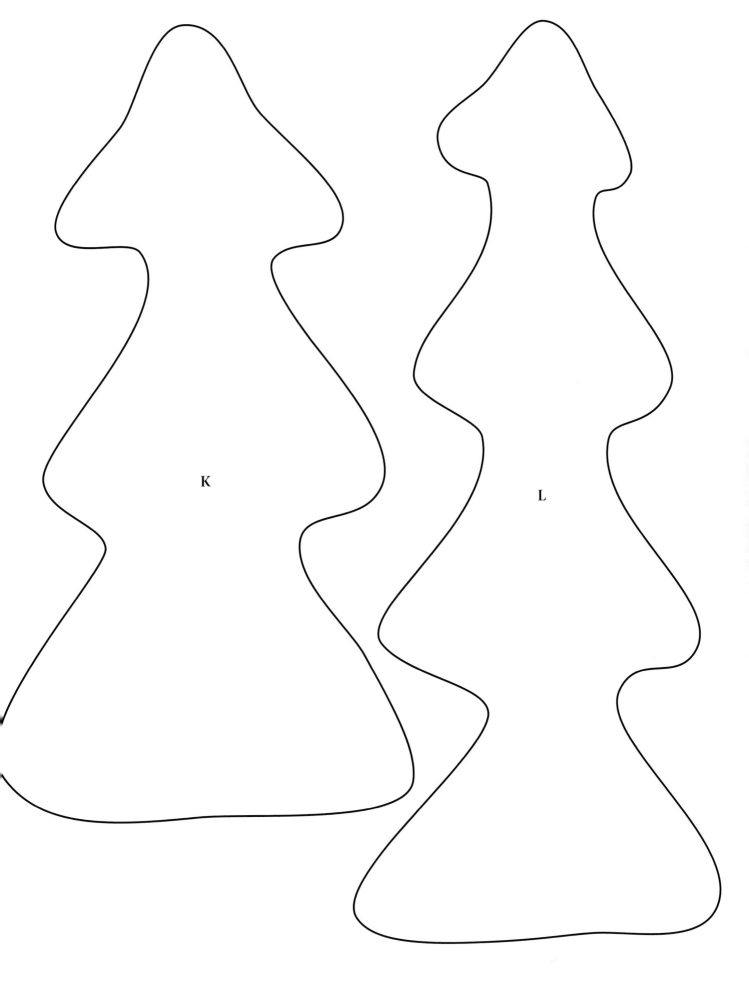

K

L

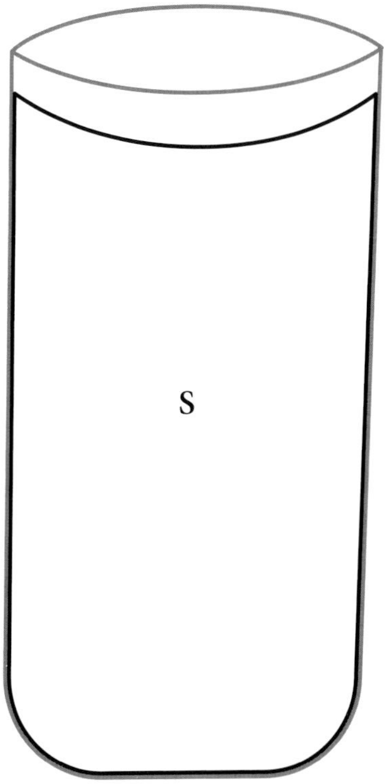

S

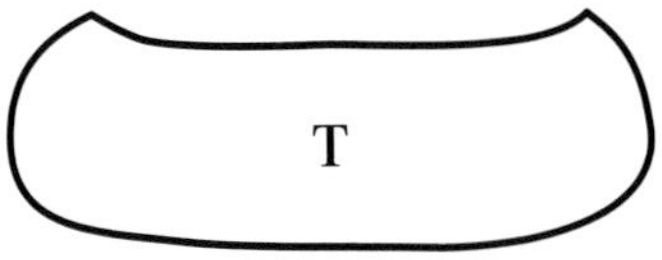

T

X

u

z

Dear Santa,
I have been
very good this
year. Please bring
me a new doll.
Hope you enjoy
the cookies and
milk. XXX

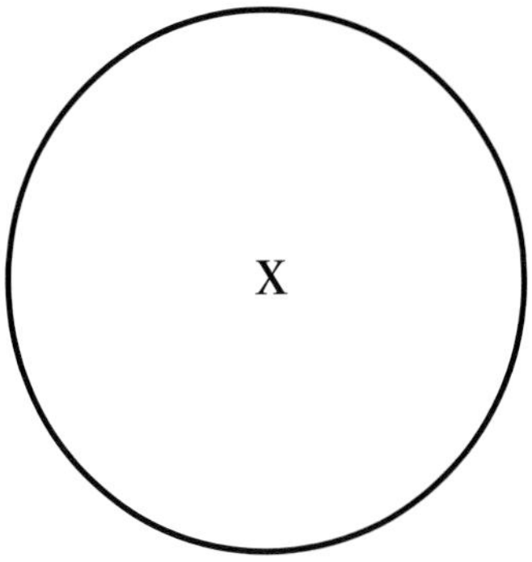

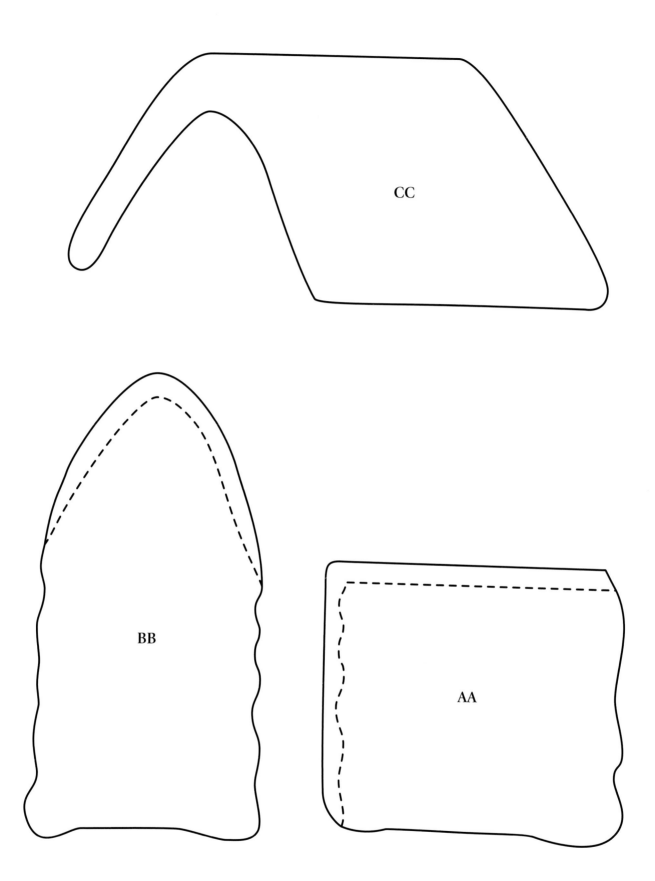

all
hearts
come
home
for

Christmas

FF

JJ

II

GG

DD

HH

EE

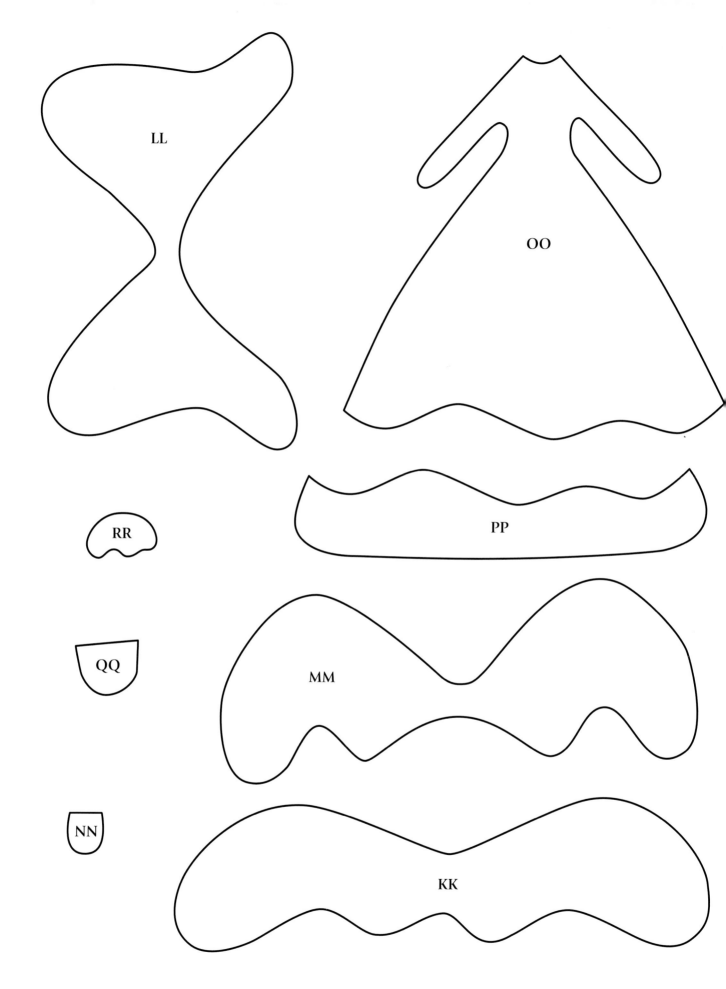

LL

OO

RR

PP

QQ

MM

NN

KK

Hi All,

I am so excited to be a part of this round robin project with all of you! The theme for my quilt is "Stars in My Sky." The key is "My." – I'd like this quilt to have a one-color background: purple (my favorite color), but not all one shade/value. A variation of purple values would be excellent. For me, purple is a neutral color! I've also opted for the details of the quilt to be in bright colors such as lime green, fuchsia, etc. Brighter fabrics seem to sizzle on a purple background. My starter block is from Pat's Star Crazy pattern which can be found in the *Best of Pat Sloan Appliqué Quilts*.

Now for a bit about me – and that could be a book in itself! I'm an eclectic soul, very grounded in my being and surroundings. My home is decorated in the things I love. I don't think I have a thing that matches or is a set. If I love something I find, it comes home with me and is worked into the decor.

I hope my journal entry gives you an idea about the "My" part of the theme. Add something that represents you so you can be a "Star in My Sky," too! Remember, purple is a neutral, at least in my world!

Happy Quilting!
Margi

stars on duty

Owner: **Margi Borck**
Machine quilted by: **Cathy Leitner**

Finished Quilt Size: 36" x 44" (91 cm x 112 cm)

MAKING THE BLOCKS

STAR WREATH BLOCK
Finished Block Size: 16" x 16" (41 cm x 41 cm)
Made by: Margi

When I started quilting, I was in a "country colors" mindset because so many patterns were presented in that colorway. But, over the years as I have gotten to know Pat, she has taught me to look "outside the box" and choose colors for my quilts that match me and my personality!

— Margi

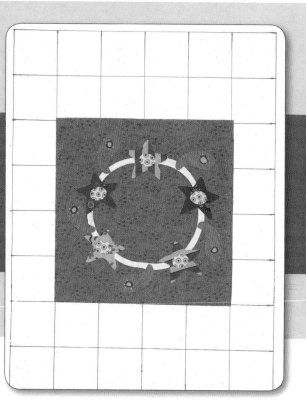

Yardage Requirements
16¹/₂" x 16¹/₂" (42 cm x 42 cm) square of purple print fabric (background)
Assorted scrap fabrics (appliqués)
You will also need:
Template plastic

Cutting Out The Pieces
From assorted scrap fabrics:
- Cut 5 wreath sections (**A**).
- Cut 5 commas (**B**).
- Cut 5 stars (**C**).
- Cut 5 star centers (**D**).

Assembling The Block
1. Work in alphabetical order to **Needle-Turn Appliqué** pieces **A – D** to background square to complete **Star Wreath Block**.

Star Wreath Block

STAR FLOWER BLOCKS

Finished Block 1 Size: 4" x 8" (10 cm x 20 cm)
Finished Block 2 Size: 12" x 8" (30 cm x 20 cm)
Made by: Pat

Margi,

I just loved working with the purple background! As soon as I saw the center block and the dragonfly on your label, I knew what I wanted to add. I love flowers, and decided a large star inside a flower would be very "me"! My buttons are embellished with a few beads for added sparkle.

The central location of your block drew me to a symmetrical setting. I asked the others what they thought and we all agreed.

You might be able to put a tiny inner border around your block, if it needs it. I sure can see a stripe there!

This has been such fun to do and I can't wait to see what Jean adds!

Pat

Note: The following 4 corner blocks are each made as 2 separate blocks. They will be sewn together and any appliqué that flows from one block to another or into the borders will be completed when assembling the quilt top.

Yardage Requirements
  10" x 10" (25 cm x 25 cm) square **each** of
    2 different purple print fabrics (background)
    Assorted scrap fabrics (appliqués)
You will also need:
    Template plastic
    3 novelty buttons
    Small beads

Cutting Out The Pieces
From *each* purple print fabric:
  - Cut 2 squares $4^1/_2$" x $4^1/_2$".
  - Cut 1 rectangle $8^1/_2$" x $4^1/_2$".

From assorted scrap fabrics:
  - Cut 3 flowers (E).
  - Cut 3 flower centers (F).
  - Cut 3 stars (G).
  - Cut 6 leaves (H).
  - Cut 2 small dragonfly wings (I).
  - Cut 2 large dragonfly wings (J).
  - Cut 2 dragonfly bodies (K).
  - Cut 5 circles (L).

Assembling The Blocks
1. Sew 2 different purple print squares together to make **Block 1**.
2. Sew the remaining 2 purple print squares and the purple print rectangles together to make **Block 2**.
3. Work in alphabetical order to **Needle-Turn Appliqué** 1 of each piece **E – G**, 2 of piece **H**, and 1 of each piece **I – L** to Block 1.

Block 1

4. Work in alphabetical order to **Needle-Turn Appliqué** 2 of each piece **E – G**, 1 of each piece **I – K**, and 4 of each piece **H** and **L** to Block 2.

Block 2

5. Sew a button, topped with a bead, to the center of each star by bringing thread up through 1 hole in button, picking up a bead and then going back down through remaining hole in button; knot off.

STAR BASKET BLOCKS
Finished Block 3 Size: 12" x 8" (30 cm x 20 cm)
Finished Block 4 Size: 4" x 8" (10 cm x 20 cm)
Made by: Jean

Margi,

Working on your quilt has been fun and has given me the opportunity to stretch beyond my comfort zone. I have always stayed away from bright colors in my fabric choices, but now may be more willing to spread my wings and try something different.

Pat's Basket of Hope Quilt from her *Folksy Favorites* book inspired my block. I liked the idea of a basket overflowing with stars. The shape of the basket was not quite right for a corner block so I used the basket from Ma-ma's garden (from the same book) and added my own star flowers.

The cute star buttons seemed to be the perfect flower centers. Special thanks to Linda Tiano, quilt designer, who suggested I piece the background with triangle-squares.

I like Pat's idea of a narrow striped border around your center block. Can't wait to see the next additions!

Jean

Yardage Requirements

12" x 12" (30 cm x 30 cm) square **each**
of 1 light and 1 dark purple print fabric
(background)
Assorted scrap fabrics (appliqués)

You will also need:

Template plastic
6 novelty buttons

Cutting Out The Pieces

From *each* purple print fabric:

- Cut 4 squares $4^7/_8$" x $4^7/_8$".

From assorted scrap fabrics:

- Cut 1 *bias* stem 1" x 12" (**M**).
- Cut 2 *bias* stems 1" x 8" (**N**).
- Cut 1 basket (**O**).
- Cut 2 small stars (**P**).
- Cut 2 small star centers (**Q**).
- Cut 4 large stars (**R**).
- Cut 4 large star centers (**S**).

Assembling The Blocks

1. Draw a diagonal line on wrong side of each light purple print square. With right sides together, place 1 light purple square on top of 1 dark purple square. Stitch $1/_4$" from each side of drawn line (**Fig. 1**).

Fig. 1

2. Cut along drawn line. Open up and press to make 2 **Triangle Squares**. Make 8 Triangle-Squares.

Triangle-Squares (make 8)

3. Sew 6 Triangle-Squares together to make **Block 3**.

4. Sew 2 Triangle-Squares together to make **Block 4**.

5. Work in alphabetical order to **Needle-Turn Appliqué** 2 of piece **N**, 1 of each piece **O - Q**, and 3 of each piece **R - S** to Block 3. *Note:* Leave an approximately $3/_4$" wide opening in top edge of basket (**O**) to insert raw end of stem (**M**) when assembling quilt top.

Block 3

6. Work in alphabetical order to **Needle-Turn Appliqué** 1 of piece **M**, and 1 of each piece **P - S** to Block 4. *Note:* The bottom end of **M** will be left free until quilt top is assembled.

Block 4

7. Sew 1 button to the center of each star.

STARS ON DUTY BLOCKS

Finished Block 5 Size: 4" x 8" (10 cm x 20 cm)
Finished Block 6 Size: 12" x 8" (30 cm x 20 cm)
Made by: Sandee

Hi Margi,

    We have never met, but I know from reading your journal that we would be instant friends!

    Pat and I had a chat and agreed that the purple background looks like a night vision so the sleeping moon and glowing stars just fell into place. "Stars on Duty" just happened when I added the moon's eyelid and smile. Who could fill the job of the moon?

    Pat's *Folksy Favorites* book influenced the shape of the moon. When I saw hers, I knew I wanted mine to have a nose. I added the ribbon bows to the stars to make them look like they were tied in the night sky! Thanks for allowing me to play. Hope you like it.

                          Sandee

Yardage Requirements

    $2^1/2$" x 20" (6 cm x 51 cm) strip **each** of 4 different purple print fabrics (Strip Set)
    Assorted scrap fabrics (appliqués)
    9" x 16" (23 cm x 41 cm) rectangle of yellow print fabric (moon)

You will also need:
    Template plastic
    Dark grey embroidery floss
    $1/2$ yd (46 cm) of $1/8$" (3 mm) wide green ribbon
    6" (15 cm) of $1/8$" (3 mm) wide gold metallic ribbon
    Air-soluble fabric marking pen

Cutting Out The Pieces

From assorted scrap fabrics:
- Cut 4 stars (**T**).
- Cut 1 sign (**U**).

From yellow print fabric:
- Cut 1 moon (**V**).

Assembling The Blocks

1. Sew 2 purple print strips together to make **Strip Set A**. Cut across Strip Set A at $2^1/2$" intervals to make 8 **Unit 1's**.

      Strip Set A   **Unit 1** (make 8)

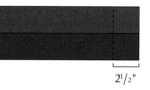

                      $2^1/2$"

2. Sew remaining purple print strips together to make **Strip Set B**. Cut across Strip Set B at $2^1/2$" intervals to make 8 **Unit 2's**.

      Strip Set B   **Unit 2** (make 8)

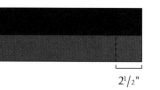

                      $2^1/2$"

3. Sew 1 Unit 1 and 1 Unit 2 together to make **Four-Patch Block**. Make 8 Four-Patch Blocks.

Four-Patch Block (make 8)

4. Sew 2 Four-Patch Blocks together to make **Block 5**.
5. Sew 6 Four-Patch Blocks together to make **Block 6**.
6. Using a light box or sunny window and air-soluble fabric pen, trace the words "Stars on Duty" onto piece **U**. Use 2 strands of floss to **Backstitch** over traced words.
7. Work in alphabetical order to **Needle-Turn Appliqué** 4 of piece **T**, piece **U**, and the top half of piece **V** to Block 6.
8. Thread a large-eye needle with metallic gold ribbon; make a knot in one end. Leaving knot showing on surface, go down through top left corner of sign and back up in background fabric, close to top edge. Take ribbon over the top of moon and go down in background fabric. Come back to surface, just under the bottom edge of moon. Go down close to top right edge of sign and back up through corner of sign. Make a knot and clip ribbon.
9. Cut green ribbon into 4 equal lengths. Tie each length into a bow. Tack 1 bow to the center of each star.

Block 5

Block 6

MOONFLOWERS BLOCKS

Finished Block 7 Size: 12" x 8" (30 cm x 20 cm)
Finished Block 8 Size: 4" x 8" (10 cm x 20 cm)
Made by: Roseann

Hi Margi!

Well, this certainly was a challenging project for me! First off, I had no bright fabrics and you know I can't just go waltzing into any old fabric store [where I live]. All my fabrics are donated from my pals so there's a little of them in this, too.

The fabrics for the background I found when I was trying to find something else — you know how that goes! It was a cute little bundle of four fat eighths. I knew I wanted to use them all so a split rail block came to mind for the background. We started calling the flowers "moon flowers" for some reason. I started doodling on paper and what came up was kind of "back to the 60s." I used to have stuff like this on my walls as a teenager!

It's been fun getting to know you through this adventure of Pat's. Maybe someday we'll meet in person. Enjoy your quilt. All my best to you!

Roseann

Yardage Requirements

1½" x 36" (4 cm x 91 cm) strip **each** of
  4 different purple print fabrics (Strip Set)
8" x 8" (20 cm x 20 cm) square **each** of blue,
  green, and aqua print fabrics
Assorted scrap fabrics (appliqués)

You will also need:
  Template plastic
  Purple embroidery floss

Cutting Out The Pieces

*Note: When cutting out appliqué piece CC,
do not add seam allowances.*

From *each* blue, green, and aqua print fabric:

- Cut 1 petal (**W**).
- Cut 2 petals (**X**).
- Cut 2 petals (**Y**).
- Cut 1 petal (**Z**).

From assorted scrap fabrics:

- Cut 3 circles (**AA**).
- Cut 3 dots (**BB**).
- Cut 3 stars (**CC**).

Assembling The Block

1. Sew 4 different purple print strips together
    to make **Strip Set**. Cut across Strip Set at
    4½" intervals to make 8 **Unit 1's**.

Strip Set **Unit 1** (make 8)

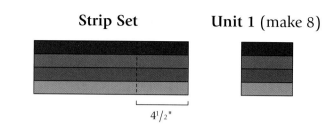

4½"

2. Alternating orientation of the strips, sew
    6 Unit 1's together to make **Block 7**.
3. Alternating orientation of the strips, sew
    2 Unit 1's together to make **Block 8**.
4. Working in alphabetical order, **Needle-Turn
    Appliqué** pieces **W – BB** to Blocks 7 and 8.
5. Use 2 strands of floss to **Blanket Stitch** 1 piece
    CC to the center of each moonflower.

Block 7 **Block 8**

When finishing my quilt, I knew I wanted to
add an inner border and the bright purple "bubble"
print I chose makes all the appliqués sing! Then,
I thought and thought about an outer border
fabric and all of a sudden it hit me — Pat's
purple fabric with gold stars would be perfect,
and it was!

— Margi

MAKING THE QUILT TOP

Sashings and Borders
Yardage Requirements
$^3/_8$ yd (34 cm) of purple print fabric (inner and middle borders)

1 yd (91 cm) of plum print fabric (outer and border binding)

3 yds (2.7 m) of backing fabric

You will also need:

44" x 52" (112 cm x 132 cm) rectangle of batting

Cutting Out The Pieces
From purple print fabric:
- Cut 2 inner side borders 1" x $15^1/_2$".
- Cut 2 inner top/bottom borders 1" x $16^1/_2$".
- Cut 2 middle side borders 2" x $32^1/_2$".
- Cut 2 middle top/bottom borders 2" x $27^1/_2$".

From plum print fabric:
- Cut 4 outer borders $4^1/_2$" x $35^1/_2$".
- Cut 5 binding strips $2^1/_4$" wide.

Assembling The Quilt Top Center
*Refer to **Quilt Top Center Diagram** for placement.*
1. Trim Star Wreath Block to $15^1/_2$" x $15^1/_2$".
2. Sew side then top/bottom inner borders to Star Wreath Block.
3. Sew Blocks 6 and 7 together to make **Row 1**.
4. Sew Blocks 5 and 4 together to make **Unit 1**. Sew Blocks 1 and 8 together to make **Unit 2**.
5. Sew Unit 1, Star Wreath Block, and Unit 2 together to make **Row 2**.
6. Sew Blocks 3 and 2 together to make **Row 3**.
7. Pin any appliqués that flow from one block to another out of the way. Stitch Rows together to make **Quilt Top Center**.

Quilt Top Center

Unit 1

Unit 2

Adding The Borders

1. Pin any appliqués that flow into the borders out of the way. Match centers and corners and sew side then top/bottom middle borders to quilt top center.
2. Repeat Step 1 to sew outer borders to quilt top center to complete **Quilt Top**.

COMPLETING THE QUILT

1. Un-pin, arrange, and finish stitching appliqués in place.
2. Follow **Quilting**, page 117, to mark, layer, and quilt as desired. Our quilt is machine quilted with outline quilting around each appliqué. There is a loose meandering pattern in the background and widely spaced feathers in the borders.
3. Follow **Making Straight-Grain Binding** and **Pat's Machine-Sewn Binding**, page 121, to bind quilt using **binding strips**.

Quilt Top Diagram

Margi's Creamy Fruit Salad
  Variety of fresh fruits, washed and cut into
    bite-size pieces. My favorites are:
        Strawberries
        Blackberries
        Blueberries
        Bananas
        Kiwi fruit
        Apples
        Nectarines
        Red and green grapes
  1 large can pineapple chunks, drained (reserve
    1 tbsp. of juice)
  1 (8 oz.) package of cream cheese
  1 small carton of sour cream
  1 tsp. vanilla
  1/3 cup granulated sugar
In a large mixing bowl, combine pineapple juice,
cream cheese, sour cream, vanilla, and sugar.
Mix until smooth and creamy. Add fruit and
toss to coat well. Refrigerate. Serve cold.

B

E

D

C

A

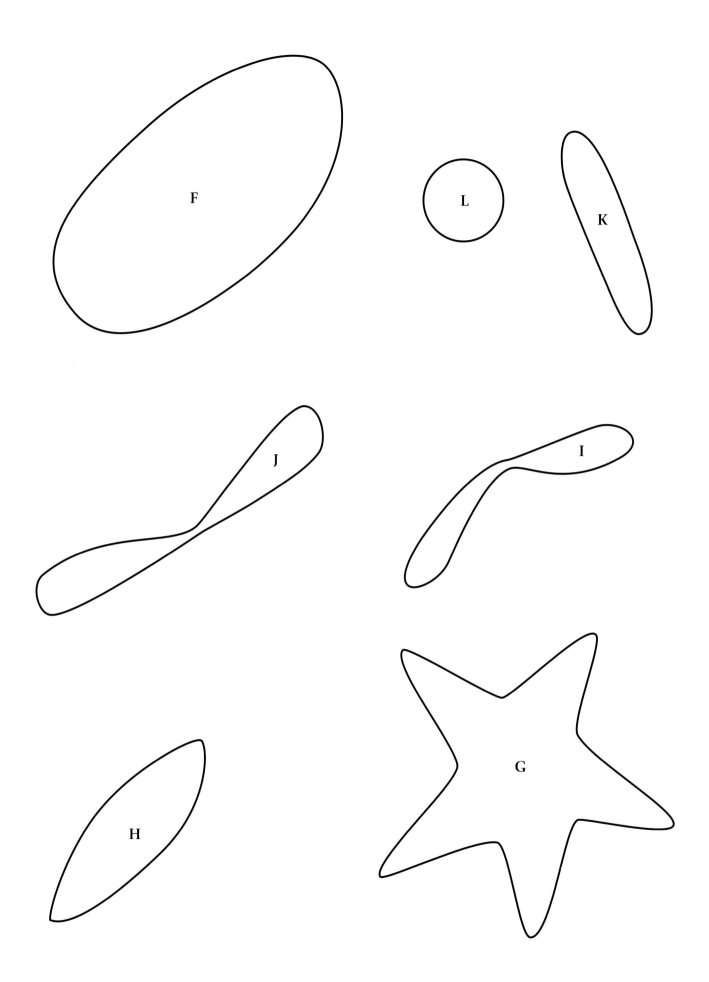

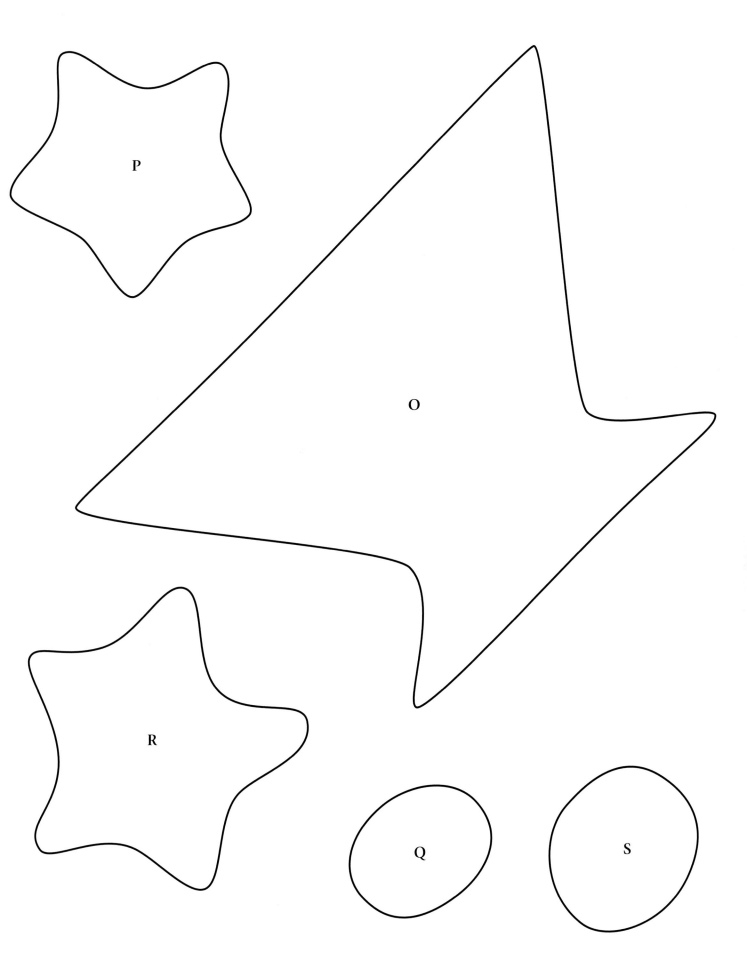

Stars On Duty

T

W

X

Z

Y

AA

CC

44

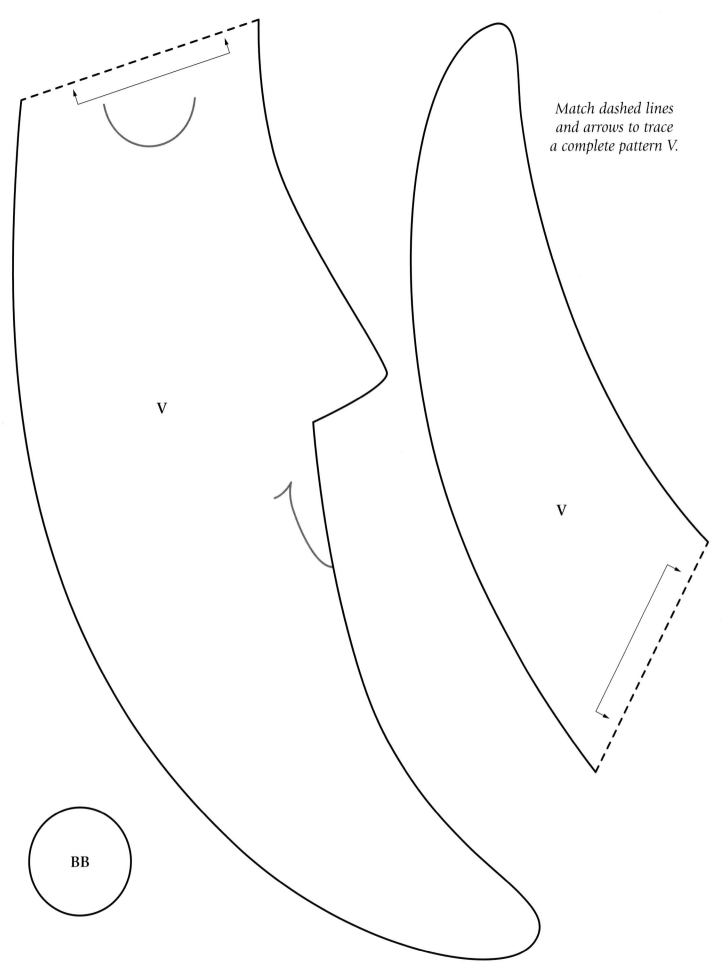

Match dashed lines and arrows to trace a complete pattern V.

V

V

BB

45

SHADES *of* AUTUMN

Owner: **Sandee Wachal**
Machine quilted by: **Joyce Robinson**

Finished Quilt Size: 40" x 50" (102 cm x 127 cm)

Greetings fellow grid players,

What a delight this project has already been for me! I can hardly wait to receive yours.

I would like the theme for my quilt to be "Shades of Autumn." This has always been my favorite time of the year since I was a kid growing up on a Minnesota farm. To this day, pretty shades of red-rust-mustard gold remind me of the maple and oak trees in our yard. And the deep shades of pine green and aspen gold here in Colorado thrill me.

For subject matter, I want you to think back to fall memories for you. Think about playing in piles of fall leaves, Halloween to Thanksgiving time. I love pumpkins, crows, Indian corn, crescent moons, and stars.

Please use flannel and woven cottons for my quilt blocks. And felted wool, please. My grapevine wreath block is made of all three. I'm including some pieces of felted wool with my grid and journal. Thanks for allowing me to play. May your needles always be filled with happy stitches!

Sandee

MAKING THE BLOCKS

WREATH BLOCK

Finished Block Size: 12" x 16" (30 cm x 41 cm)
Made by: Sandee

We were all awestruck by Sandee's workmanship, choice of colors, and use of fabrics in her Wreath Block and we voted her label "the one we all wanted!"
— Pat

Yardage Requirements

Two 6¹/₂" x 8¹/₂" (17 cm x 22 cm) rectangles of cream print fabric (background)
Two 6¹/₂" x 8¹/₂" (17 cm x 22 cm) rectangles of tan print fabric (background)
³/₄" x 48" (2 cm x 122 cm) bias strip **each** of 3 different brown fabrics (vines)
4" x 12" (10 cm x 30 cm) rectangle **each** of 1 gold and 1 rust print fabric (leaves)
Assorted scraps of wool (berries)

You will also need:
Template plastic
Tan and brown No. 3 pearl cotton
¹/₄" (7 mm) wide bias tape maker (optional)
Water-soluble fabric basting glue (optional)

Cutting Out The Pieces

Note: When cutting out piece B, do not add seam allowances.

From gold and rust print fabrics:
- Cut a total of 18 leaves (**A**).

From assorted scraps of wool:
- Cut a total of 45 berries (**B**).

Assembling The Block

1. Sew background rectangles together to make **block background**.
2. To make vines, press under $^3/_{16}$" on long edges of each bias strip or follow manufacturer's instructions for using bias tape maker.
3. To make wreath, weave vines over and under each other on block background until you are pleased with the placement. So that there are no visible starting and stopping points in the wreath, hide raw ends under sections where vines cross or plan to place a leaf over raw ends. Pin or use basting glue to temporarily hold vines in place. Using a **Blindstitch,** appliqué vines to block background.
4. Arrange pieces **A** around wreath; **Needle-Turn Appliqué** in place.
5. Arrange pieces **B** around wreath. Using tan or brown pearl cotton, make 1 **Cross Stitch** through the center of each **B** to complete **Wreath Block.**

Wreath Block

VINE BLOCK

Finished Block Size: 4" x 24" (10 cm x 61 cm)

Made by: Roseann

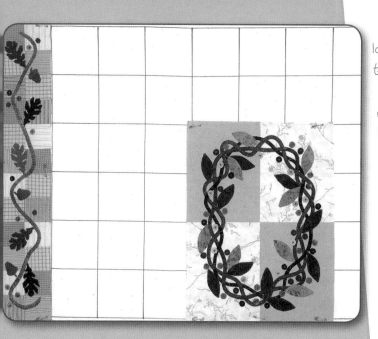

Sandee,

I can't believe how spectacular all of these quilts look! It's fun to have Internet show-and-tell as they're completed.

Like Sandee, I grew up in what was considered rural Minnesota. The countryside was rolling and hilly and covered with oak and maple trees. The color in the fall would hurt your eyes, it was so intense! I think that's why I'm drawn to those colors — pastels never interested me, but give me an autumn palette and I'm happy.

My mom maintained a 400-foot perennial bed. In the fall, the squirrels would bury acorns in the garden — drove Mom nuts when they would start to sprout the next season.

You picked a great theme, Sandee. Can't wait to see your quilt finished!

Roseann

Yardage Requirements

Assorted tan plaid, striped, and checked fabric scraps (background)

Assorted scraps of wool (appliqués)

You will also need:

Template plastic

Seed beads

Water-soluble fabric basting glue (optional)

Green and tan embroidery floss

Cutting Out The Pieces

Note: When cutting out appliqué pieces C - G, do not add seam allowances.

From assorted tan plaid, striped, and checked fabric scraps:

- Cut a total of 24 squares $2^1/2$" x $2^1/2$".

From assorted scraps of wool:

- Cut 1 vine $1/4$" x 27" (**C**).
- Cut 3 acorns (**D**).
- Cut 3 acorn caps (**E**).
- Cut 5 leaves (**F**).
- Cut 12 berries (**G**).

Assembling The Block

1. Sew 12 squares together to make a **Row**. Make 2 Rows. Sew Rows together vertically to make **block background**.
2. Arrange piece **C** on block background; pin or use basting glue to temporarily hold in place. Spacing stitches approximately $1/8$" - $1/4$" apart, use 2 strands of green floss to make **Couching Stitches** over **C**.

3. Arrange pieces **D - F** on block background; pin or use basting glue to temporarily hold pieces in place.
4. Use 1 strand of tan floss to appliqué pieces **D - F** to block background with **Straight Stitches**. Make a **Running Stitch** vein through center of each leaf.
5. Attach piece **G** by bringing thread up through center of **G**, picking up a bead, and then going back down through all layers; knot off. Repeat for each piece **G** to complete **Vine Block**.

Vine Block

50

PUMPKIN PATCH BLOCK
Finished Block Size: 12" x 12" (30 cm x 30 cm)
Made by: Margi

Sandee,

I so love your quilt and theme that I almost don't want to pass it along. As with you, fall is my favorite time of the year.

The first thing I thought of was pumpkins, and I knew Pat's from Quilt the Seasons would be the perfect addition, especially made of the scrumptious felted wool colors you provided.

As a child, I always loved Halloween and pumpkins. To this day, decorating with and carving pumpkins is one of my favorite things to do. And I know when this time comes it is soon time to feast with the family and give thanks for all that we have.

Thank you so much for the opportunity to work on your beautiful quilt and to work with a "new-to-me" medium! It was great fun!

Your friend in quilting,
Margi

Yardage Requirements

    $6^1/2$" x $6^1/2$" (17 cm x 17 cm) square of cream stripe fabric (background)

    9" x 15" (23 cm x 38 cm) rectangle of green check fabric (background)

    6" x 14" (15 cm x 36 cm) rectangle of tan plaid fabric (background)

    Assorted scraps of wool (pumpkins and stems)

    Scrap of green print fabric (leaf)

You will also need:

    Template plastic

    Brown and green embroidery floss

Cutting Out The Pieces

Note: When cutting out appliqué pieces H - M, do not add seam allowances.

From green check fabric:
- Cut one $6^1/2$" x $6^1/2$" large square.
- Cut nine $2^1/2$" x $2^1/2$" small squares.

From tan plaid fabric:
- Cut nine $2^1/2$" x $2^1/2$" small squares.

From assorted scraps of wool:
- Cut 1 of each pumpkin (**H - J**).
- Cut 1 of each pumpkin stem (**K - M**).

From scrap of green print fabric:
- Cut 1 leaf (**N**).

Assembling The Block

Use 2 strands of floss for all embroidery.

1. Sew 4 green check and 5 tan plaid small squares together to make **Nine-Patch Block A**. Sew 5 green check and 4 tan plaid small squares together to make **Nine-Patch Block B**.

Nine-Patch Block A

Nine-Patch Block B

2. Sew cream stripe and green check large squares and Nine-Patch Blocks together to make **block background**.

3. Use brown floss and work in alphabetical order to **Blanket Stitch** pieces **H - M** to block background. **Backstitch** accent lines on large pumpkin.

4. **Needle-Turn Appliqué** piece **N** to block background.

5. Use green floss to **Stem Stitch** a vine between leaf and largest pumpkin to complete **Pumpkin Patch Block**.

Pumpkin Patch Block

CHIPPIE AND STAR BLOCKS

Finished Chippie Block Size: 12" x 12" (30 cm x 30 cm)
Finished Star Block Size: 4" x 8" (10 cm x 20 cm)
Made by: Pat

Sandee,

As soon as I saw your project, I thought of Fall. I wanted to add something that would be your favorite, so I thought and thought. Then as the months went along it came to me – I had to add "Chippie." Your pet chipmunk at your cabin would be a perfect addition.

I drew up a few designs, then worried how they would look in fabric. I'm happy to say that the final chipmunk is as I hoped! And she had to be chubby since you feed her so-o-o many peanuts, ha-ha! The Chippie on the block is gathering acorns for the winter coming up, but we know your Chippie will continue to be well fed!

Much love and friendship,
Pat

Yardage Requirements

Two 6^1/$_2$" x 6^1/$_2$" (17 cm x 17 cm) squares **each** of 2 cream print fabrics (Chippie background)

4^1/$_2$" x 8^1/$_2$" (11 cm x 22 cm) rectangle of tan print fabric (star background)

1" x 28" (3 cm x 71 cm) bias strip of green print fabric (vine)

Assorted scrap fabrics (appliqués)

Assorted scraps of wool (leaves and berries)

You will also need:

Template plastic

Brown variegated and yellow No. 3 pearl cotton

Water-soluble fabric basting glue (optional)

Cutting Out The Pieces

*Note: When cutting out appliqué pieces **AA - DD**, do not add seam allowances.*

From assorted scrap fabrics:

- Cut 2 outer ears (**O**).
- Cut 1 chipmunk (**P**).
- Cut 1 inner ear (**Q**).
- Cut 2 acorns (**R**).
- Cut 2 acorn caps (**S**).
- Cut 1 acorn stem (**T**).
- Cut 1 of each stripe (**U - V**).
- Cut 1 hind leg (**W**).
- Cut 1 front leg (**X**).
- Cut 1 tail (**Y**).
- Cut 2 stars (**Z**).

From assorted scraps of wool:

- Cut 1 eye (**AA**).
- Cut 3 leaves (**BB**).
- Cut 9 berries (**CC**).
- Cut 2 star centers (**DD**).

Assembling The Blocks

1. Sew 4 cream background squares together to make **Chippie background**.
2. Arrange vine on Chippie background; pin or use basting glue to temporarily hold vine in place. **Needle-Turn Appliqué** vine to Chippie background.
3. Work in alphabetical order to **Needle-Turn Appliqué** 1 piece **O**, piece **P**, remaining piece **O**, and pieces **Q – Y** to Chippie background.

4. Use brown variegated pearl cotton to **Blanket Stitch** around pieces **AA – CC**, and to make **Straight Stitch** whiskers and eye details on chipmunk to complete **Chippie Block**.

Chippie Block

5. **Needle-Turn Appliqué** pieces **Z** to the star background. Use yellow pearl cotton to **Blanket Stitch** 1 **DD** to the center of each star to complete **Star Block**.

Star Block

PUMPKIN AND AUTUMN BLOCKS

Finished Pumpkin Block Size: 8" x 8" (20 cm x 20 cm)
Finished Autumn Block Size: 4" x 24" (10 cm x 61 cm)
Made by: Jean

Hi Sandee,

Your quilt is just beautiful! Being the last to work on it was an advantage as I got to see in person all the stunning blocks and pull ideas from them.

There can never be too many pumpkins in a fall garden, so I thought you needed one more pumpkin. And even though it is obvious your quilt has a fall theme, the word "Autumn" seemed to balance Roseann's vine. The buttons are just barely attached so you can remove them to piece the quilt. I also included the rest of the package of buttons, just in case you wanted to arrange them differently.

After the HOT and HUMID days of summer in the South, the cool fall air is always a welcome change.

Thanks for letting me play and get to know you in the process.

Happy Quilting,
Jean

Yardage Requirements

$8^1/_2$" x $8^1/_2$" (22 cm x 22 cm) square of cream print fabric (pumpkin background)

$4^1/_2$" x $4^1/_2$" (11 cm x 11 cm) square **each** of 6 different tan plaid or stripe fabrics (autumn background)

1" x 32" (3 cm x 81 cm) bias strip of green print fabric

Scrap of green fabric (leaf)

$6^1/_2$" x $6^1/_2$" (17 cm x 17 cm) square of orange wool (pumpkin)

7" x 10" (18 cm x 25 cm) rectangle of brown wool (pumpkin stem and letters)

You will also need:
Template plastic
Water-soluble fabric basting glue (optional)
Brown variegated wool floss
Brown No. 3 pearl cotton
6 novelty buttons

Cutting Out The Pieces

Note: When cutting out appliqué pieces FF, GG, and AUTUMN, do not add seam allowances.

From green fabric:
- Cut 1 leaf (EE).

From orange wool:
- Cut 1 pumpkin (FF).

From brown wool:
- Cut 1 pumpkin stem (GG).
- Cut letters to spell AUTUMN.

Assembling The Blocks

1. **Needle-Turn Appliqué** piece EE to pumpkin background.
2. Use brown pearl cotton to **Blanket Stitch** pieces FF and GG to pumpkin background. *Note:* Leave an approximately ³/₄" wide opening in the top of FF for inserting vine end when assembling quilt top.
3. Use brown pearl cotton to **Stem Stitch** a stem on leaf and **Backstitch** accent lines on pumpkin to complete **Pumpkin Block**.

Pumpkin Block

4. Sew 6 tan background squares together to make **autumn background**.
5. Leaving approximately 5" of vine extending off left edge of fabric, arrange vine on autumn background; pin or use basting glue to temporarily hold vine in place. **Needle-Turn Appliqué** vine to autumn background.
6. Use brown varigated wool floss to **Blanket Stitch** letters AUTUMN to autumn background. Sew buttons to vine to complete **Autumn Block**.

Autumn Block

To finish my quilt, I considered adding sashings with corner posts, borders, and appliquéd wool leaves in a couple of border corners. After studying the grid pinned to my design wall, I decided against the appliqués and chose to use pieced sashings. I finished it with a double border.
— Sandee

MAKING THE QUILT TOP

Sashings and Borders

Yardage Requirements

¹/₈ yd (11 cm) **each** of gold, red, green, and brown print fabrics (sashing).

1⁵/₈ yds (1.5 m) of gold stripe fabric (inner border)

1⁵/₈ yds (1.5 m) of brown plaid fabric (outer border and binding)

2³/₄ yds (2.5 m) of backing fabric

You will also need:

48" x 58" (122 cm x 147 cm) rectangle of batting

Cutting Out The Pieces

From gold, red, green, and brown print fabrics:

- Cut a *total* of 231 squares 1¹/₂" x 1¹/₂".

From gold stripe fabric:

- Cut 2 *lengthwise* inner top/bottom borders 2¹/₂" x 53".
- Cut 2 *lengthwise* inner side borders 2¹/₂" x 43".

From brown plaid fabric:

- Cut 2 *lengthwise* outer top/bottom borders 4¹/₂" x 53".
- Cut 2 *lengthwise* outer side borders 4¹/₂" x 43".
- Cut 1 binding square 22" x 22".

Assembling The Quilt Top Center

*Refer to **Assembly Diagram**, page 58, when making the quilt top center.*

1. Sew 4 squares together to make **sashing strip A**. Make 2 A's. Sew 1 A to the top of Vine Block and 1 to the bottom of Autumn Block.

Vine Block   **Autumn Block**

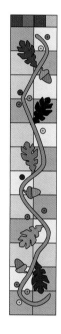 

2. Sew 12 squares together to make **sashing strip B**. Make 2 B's. Sew 1 B to the top of the Pumpkin Patch and Wreath Blocks. Sew 17 squares together to make **sashing strip C**. Sew C to right side of Wreath Block.

Pumpkin Patch Block   **Wreath Block**

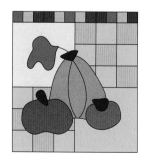 

3. Sew 8 squares together to make **sashing strip D**. Sew **D** to the right side of Star Block.

Star Block

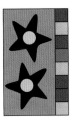

4. Sew 25 squares together to make **sashing strip E**. Make 4 **E**'s.
5. Sew Vine Block, 1 **E**, Chippie Block, and Pumpkin Patch Block together to make **Unit 1**.

Unit 1

6. Sew Star, Pumpkin, and Wreath Blocks together to make **Unit 2**.

Unit 2

7. Sew Autumn Block to the right side of Unit 2 to make **Unit 3**.

Unit 3

8. Sew 37 squares together to make **sashing strip F**. Make 2 **F**'s.
9. Referring to **Assembly Diagram**, page 58, sew Unit 1, 3 **E**'s, Unit 3, and 2 **F**'s together.
10. Insert raw end of vine into opening in top of **GG**. **Blanket Stitch** across opening of **GG** to complete **Quilt Top Center**.

Adding Mitered Borders

Fig. 1

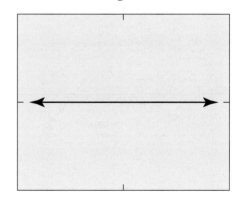

1. Matching long edges, sew inner and outer side borders together. Repeat with top/bottom inner and outer borders.
2. Mark the center of each edge of quilt top center and each border.
3. Measure across the center of quilt top (**Fig. 1**). Matching center marks and raw edges, pin top border to quilt top center. Beginning at center of border, measure $^1/_2$ the width of the quilt top center in both directions and mark. Match marks on border with corners of quilt top center and pin. Easing in any fullness, pin border to quilt top center between center and corners. Beginning and ending seams exactly $^1/_4$" from each corner of quilt top center and back stitching at beginning and end of stitching, sew top border to quilt top center (**Fig. 2**).

Fig. 2

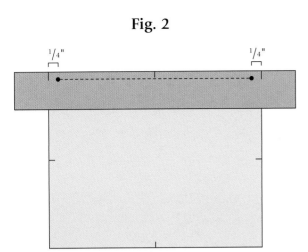

4. Repeat Step 3 to sew bottom and then side borders to quilt top center. To temporarily move first 2 borders out of the way, fold and pin ends as shown in **Fig. 3**.

Fig. 3

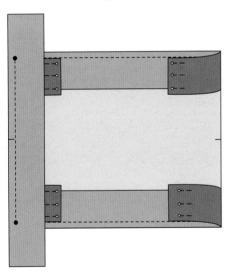

5. Fold 1 corner of quilt top center diagonally with right sides together and matching edges. Use a ruler to mark stitching line as shown in **Fig. 4**. Pin borders together along drawn line. Sew on drawn line, backstitching at beginning and end of stitching (**Fig. 5**).

Fig. 4

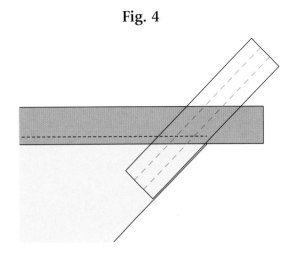

Fig. 5

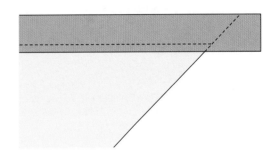

6. Turn mitered corner right side up. Check to make sure corner lies flat with no gaps or puckers.

7. Trim seam allowance to $^1/_4$"; press to 1 side.

8. Repeat Steps 5 - 7 to miter each remaining corner.

COMPLETING THE QUILT

1. Follow **Quilting**, page 117, to mark, layer, and quilt as desired. Our quilt is machine quilted with outline quilting around each appliqué and meander quilting in the block backgrounds. Each sashing square is quilted with an X. The inner border is quilted with straight lines and the outer border is quilted with a leaf pattern.

2. Use binding square and follow **Making Continuous Bias Binding**, page 120, to make $2^1/_4$" wide binding. Follow **Attaching Binding With Mitered Corners**, page 122, to bind quilt.

Quilt Top Diagram

Sandee's Rice Casserole

- 1 cup cooked wild rice
- 2 cups cooked brown rice
- 1 can sliced water chestnuts
- 1 lb cooked Italian sausage
- 1/2 cup slivered almonds
- 1/2 cup chopped celery
- 1/2 cup chopped carrots
- 1/2 cup chopped onions
- 1/2 cup chopped green peppers
- 1 can corn (drained)
- 1 can cream of mushroom soup

Mix all ingredients together. Place in a greased baking dish. Bake 1 hour at 350°. Double for company. Serve with a green salad and warm rolls.

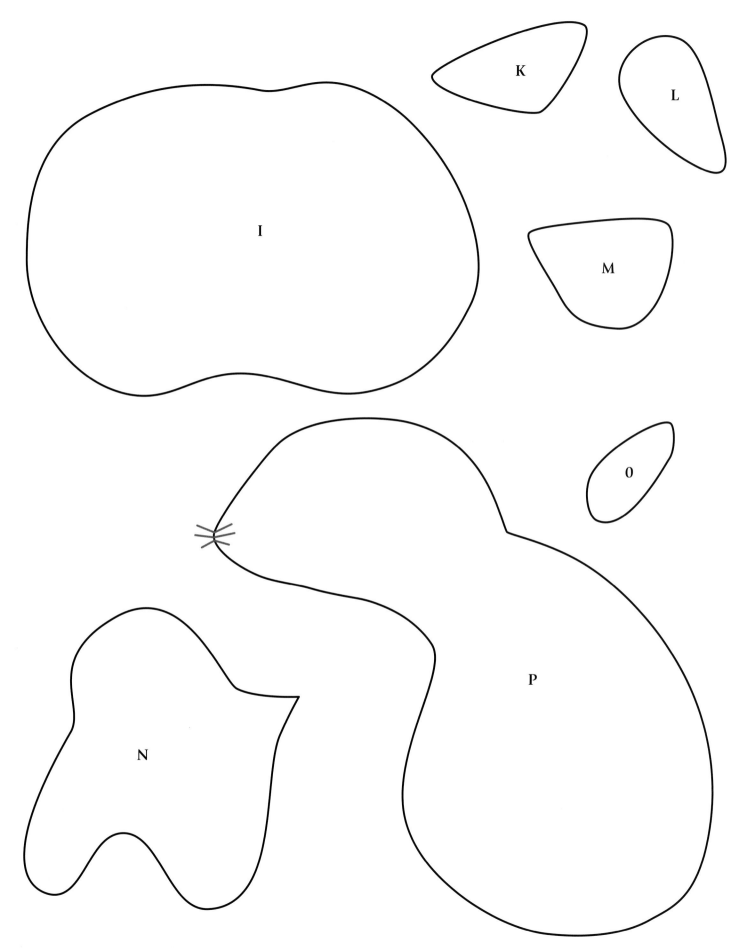

AA

CC

DD

EE

BB

FF

GG

Hi Sandee, Margi, Pat, and Roseann,

Ocean breezes, saltwater spray, sailboats and lighthouses. My love affair with the ocean and all things nautical started in my childhood, which was spent growing up in Charleston, South Carolina. It is a passion that has stayed with me throughout my adult life.

I invite you to join me on this ocean voyage with your interpretation of a nautical block. Mariner's Compasses, Storm at Sea Blocks, lighthouses — what comes to mind when you think of the ocean?

As you can see, I like homespun fabrics and darker colors. Please feel free to use some of my scraps or choose your own fabrics. I look forward to seeing what each of you comes up with and having a quilt that was made by a circle of friends.

Jean

SMOOTH *sailing*

Owner: **Jean Lewis**
Machine quilted by: **Julie Schrader**

Finished Quilt Size: 35" x 43" (89 cm x 109 cm)

MAKING THE BLOCKS

SAILBOAT BLOCK
Finished Block Size: 12" x 16" (30 cm x 41 cm)
Made by: Jean

Designing this block was so much fun! I started with the striped fabric, from Pat's Old Blooms collection. And, although I am already in the race for who has the biggest stash, this block "required" a trip to both of my local quilt stores to find just the right fabrics — any excuse for a shopping spree!

— Jean

Yardage Requirements
9¹/₂" x 16¹/₂" (24 cm x 42 cm) rectangle of navy plaid fabric (background)
3¹/₂" x 16¹/₂" (9 cm x 42 cm) rectangle of blue stripe fabric (background)
Assorted scrap fabrics (appliqués)

Cutting Out The Pieces
From assorted scrap fabrics:
- Cut 1 of each sail (**A - C**).
- Cut 1 flag (**D**).
- Cut 1 mast (**E**).
- Cut 1 boom (**F**).
- Cut 1 hull trim (**G**).
- Cut 1 hull (**H**).
- Cut 1 moon (**I**).
- Cut 1 star (**J**).
- Cut 1 of each letter **SAIL**.

Assembling The Block

1. Sew rectangles together to make **block background**.
2. *Note: Appliqué hull trim G to hull H, before appliquéing hull H to background.*
   Work in alphabetical order to **Needle-Turn Appliqué** pieces **A – J** and the letters **SAIL** to block background to complete **Sailboat Block**.

Sailboat Block

STORM AT SEA BLOCK
Finished Block Size: 16" x 8" (41 cm x 20 cm)
Made by: Sandee

Happy New Year, Jean!

Hope this is a good year for all the grid group. Love your nautical theme! It also brings happy childhood memories for me. I grew up on a farm in Minnesota but my folks loved to travel. Our favorite vacation spot was Galveston, Texas. My happiest memories of being with my dad was when we walked the beach early in the morning, picking up sea shells.

So I did a couple of Storm at Sea blocks to fit under your sailboat. I just felt like I needed to get that boat into the water! I spent a weekend and then a couple of evenings in Denver looking for some fish to sew on but didn't find any. Colorado is a little short on nautical décor! Finally, I walked into our local craft store and there were the fish, and even in the right color. Now you have a school of fish swimming in the waves. Hope you like them.

Sandee

Yardage Requirements

$^1/_4$ yd (23 cm) of blue solid fabric
$^1/_4$ yd (23 cm) of navy print fabric

You will also need:
Template plastic
Novelty buttons

Cutting Out The Pieces

From blue solid fabric:
- Cut 1 strip $2^1/_2$" wide. From this strip, cut 8 large squares $2^1/_2$" x $2^1/_2$" and 8 small squares 2" x 2".
- Cut 32 of template (**K**).

From navy print fabric:
- Cut 1 strip $3^3/_8$" wide. From this strip, cut 2 large squares $3^3/_8$" x $3^3/_8$" and 4 medium squares $2^7/_8$" x $2^7/_8$". Cut each medium square in half once diagonally to make 8 triangles.
- Cut 2 strips $1^1/_2$" wide. From these strips, cut 32 small squares $1^1/_2$" x $1^1/_2$".
- Cut 8 of template (**L**).

Assembling The Block

1. Place 1 navy print small square on one corner of 1 blue solid large square and stitch diagonally (**Fig. 1**). Trim $^1/_4$" from stitching line (**Fig. 2**). Open up and press seam allowances toward darker fabric (**Fig. 3**).

Fig. 1

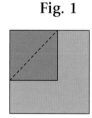

Fig. 2

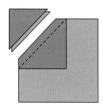

Fig. 3

2. Repeat Step 1 to sew 1 navy print small square to each remaining corner of the blue solid large square to make 1 **Corner Unit**. Make 8 Corner Units.

Corner Unit (make 8)

3. Using navy print large and blue solid small squares, repeat Steps 1 and 2 to make **Unit 1**. Make 2 Unit 1's.

Unit 1 (make 2)

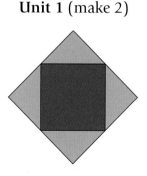

4. Sew 1 navy print triangle to each side of 1 Unit 1 to make **Center Unit**. Make 2 Center Units.

Center Unit (make 2)

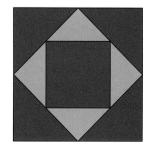

5. With right sides together, match dots to sew 1 **K** to each side of an **L** to make **Diamond Unit**. Make 8 Diamond Unit's.

Diamond Unit (make 8)

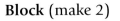

6. Sew 1 Center Unit, 4 Corner Units, and 4 Diamond Units together to make **Block**. Make 2 Blocks.

Block (make 2)

7. Sew 2 Blocks together to make **Storm At Sea Block**. Arrange, and then sew buttons to block.

Storm At Sea Block

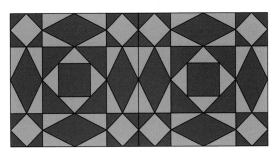

KITE BLOCK
Finished Block Size: 12" x 12" (30 cm x 30 cm)
Made by: Margi

Hi Jean,

Your grid presented quite a challenge for me as I am not a water person at all. But the wonderful memories of my teen years came springing back for me. Although I never touched the water, I do have fond memories of my friends and I flying our handmade kites at our local lake hang-out. I think the most fun for me was the construction of our kites. They didn't always fly, but they always turned out beautifully.

The kite I added is my own creation with one of Pat's flowers in the center. Of course I had to add my two favorites, purple and sunflowers!

Enjoy!
Margi

71

Yardage Requirements

12¹/₂" x 12¹/₂" (32 cm x 32 cm) square of blue print fabric (background)

5¹/₂" x 10¹/₂" (14 cm x 27 cm) rectangle **each** of red stripe and red print fabric (kite)

Assorted scrap fabrics (appliqués)

You will also need:

Template plastic

2 novelty buttons

12" (30 cm) of black baby rickrack

Water-soluble fabric basting glue (optional)

Cutting Out The Pieces

From *each* red stripe and red print fabric:

- Cut one 4¹/₂" x 5¹/₂" and one 4¹/₂" x 6¹/₂" rectangle.

From assorted scrap fabrics:

- Cut 1 leaf (**N**). Cut 1 leaf in reverse (**Nr**).
- Cut 1 flower (**O**).
- Cut 1 flower center (**P**).
- Cut 2 kite bows (**Q**).

Assembling The Block

1. Sew the 4 kite rectangles together (**Fig. 4**). Make a template from pattern **M**. Place template over the sewn rectangle, matching dashed lines on template with seams in rectangle. Follow **Template Cutting**, page 115, to cut out kite (**M**).

Fig. 4

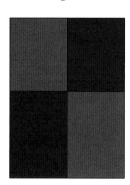

2. Work in alphabetical order to arrange and pin appliqué pieces **M** - **P** on background.
3. Tuck one raw end of rickrack under bottom point of **M**. Pin or use basting glue to temporarily hold rickrack; machine straight stitch in place. Pin pieces **Q** on top of rickrack.
4. **Needle-Turn Appliqué** pieces **M** - **Q** to background.
5. Sew 1 button to center of each **Q** to complete **Kite Block**.

Kite Block

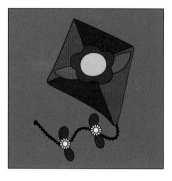

LIGHTHOUSE AND STAR BLOCKS

Finished Lighthouse Block Size: 8" x 20" (20 cm x 51 cm)
Finished Star Block Size: 4" x 12" (10 cm x 30 cm)
Made by: Pat

Jean,

As soon as I read your foreword, I knew I wanted to do a lighthouse! As a child, I lived a few blocks from the Atlantic Ocean in New Jersey. We spent many summer days playing at the beach. As I got ready to work on your block, our trip to Florida came up. Your block took a lovely, warm vacation in February!

We visited St. Augustine, Florida and climbed the lighthouse; your block enjoyed that, too! I can't wait to see the finished quilt. Thank you so much for being in the robin!

Pat

Yardage Requirements

8^1/$_2$" x 16^1/$_2$" (22 cm x 42 cm) rectangle of blue plaid fabric (lighthouse background)

8^1/$_2$"x 4^1/$_2$" (22 cm x 11 cm) rectangle of navy print fabric (lighthouse background)

4^1/$_2$" x 12^1/$_2$" (11 cm x 32 cm) rectangle of navy print fabric (star background)

Assorted scrap fabrics (appliqués)

You will also need:

Template plastic

Cutting Out The Pieces

From assorted scrap fabrics:

- Cut 1 light (**R**).
- Cut 1 roof (**S**).
- Cut 1 of each lighthouse stripe (**T - X**).
- Cut 4 windows (**Y**).
- Cut 1 star (**Z**).
- Cut 1 of each letter **TO**

Assembling The Blocks

1. Sew lighthouse background rectangles together to make **block background**.
2. Work in alphabetical order to arrange and pin pieces **R – Y** to block background. **Needle-Turn Appliqué** pieces in place to complete **Lighthouse Block**.

Lighthouse Block

3. **Needle-Turn Appliqué** piece **Z** and the letters **TO** to the star background to complete **Star Block**.

Star Block

WEATHERVANE BLOCK
Finished Block Size: 12" x 8" (30 cm x 20 cm)
Made by: Roseann

Hey Jean!

Your quilt was a lot of fun for me. Well, the appliqué part of it wasn't such a blast, but the theme was!

I received your quilt with the last section to fill. It seemed like all the good ideas were taken. But one day, I came across a weathervane and I knew that was the answer! The sailboat had to know which direction the wind was coming from, didn't it? I quickly drew a weathervane that would have a whale rather than the traditional rooster.

Your whole quilt moves me back to the East Coast in my mind. I was stationed in Virginia during the military and never got tired of going out to the ocean or to Yorktown and the river to watch the activity there. In many ways, your quilt is a memory quilt for me!

I'm so glad I had this opportunity to work with you on the grid quilts. I hope some day to meet you in person. It's been fun getting to know you online.

All my best,
Roseann

Yardage Requirements
$12^1/_2$" x $8^1/_2$" (32 cm x 22 cm) rectangle
of blue stripe fabric (background)
Assorted scrap fabrics (appliqués)
You will also need:
Template plastic

Cutting Out The Pieces
From assorted scrap fabrics:
- Cut 1 stand (**AA**).
- Cut 1 whale (**BB**).
- Cut 1 arrow (**CC**).
- Cut 1 circle (**DD**).
- Cut 1 star (**EE**).

Assembling The Block
1. Working in alphabetical order, **Needle-Turn Appliqué** pieces **AA** – **EE** to background to complete **Weathervane Block**.

Weathervane Block

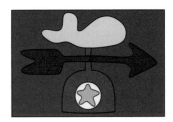

Originally, I had not planned to use borders on my quilt and wanted to hand quilt it. After piecing the top I decided that the boat might sail into the sunset and the kite might fly away without borders to contain them! And then, after the top was all sewn together, I couldn't resist using the talents of our awesome machine quilter!
— Jean

Sashings and Borders

Yardage Requirements

    $12^1/2$" x $1^1/2$" (32 cm x 4 cm) strip of red plaid fabric (sashing)

    1 yd (91 cm) of gold print fabric (inner border)

    $^7/_8$ yd (80 cm) of navy blue print fabric (outer border and binding)

    3 yds (2.7 m) of backing fabric

You will also need:

    43" x 51" (109 cm x 130 cm) rectangle of batting

Cutting Out The Pieces

From gold print fabric:

- Cut 2 inner top/bottom borders $1^1/2$" x $26^1/2$".
- Cut 2 inner side borders $1^1/2$" x $32^1/2$".

From navy print fabric:

- Cut 2 outer top/bottom borders $4^1/2$" x $34^1/2$".
- Cut 2 outer side borders $4^1/2$" x $34^1/2$".
- Cut 5 binding strips $2^1/4$" wide.

Assembling The Quilt Top Center

*Refer to **Quilt Top Diagram**, page 78, for placement.*

1. Trim $^1/2$" from bottom edge of Kite Block and $^1/2$" from top edges of Lighthouse and Star Blocks. Sew sashing strip to bottom edge of Kite Block.

2. With top edges even, sew Lighthouse and Star Blocks together, stopping and backstitching $^1/4$" from bottom edge of Star Block as shown in **Fig. 5** to make **Unit 1**.

Fig. 5   **Unit 1**

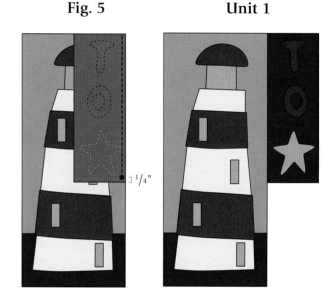

$^1/4$"

3. Sew Kite Block and Unit 1 together to make **Unit 2**.

4. Sew Weathervane and Sailboat Blocks together to make **Unit 3**.

5. With top edges even, sew Units 2 and 3 together to make **Unit 4**.

Unit 4

6. On wrong side of Storm At Sea Block, mark a dot ¹/₄" from each edge of bottom left corner.

7. With right sides of Storm at Sea Block and Unit 4 together, match dot and end of seam between Star Block and Lighthouse Block; pin edges together. Begin stitching at outer edge and stitch to dot (indicated in pink); backstitch, remove pins, and clip threads (**Fig. 6**).

Fig. 6

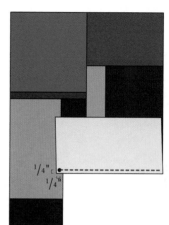

8. To sew seam between Storm At Sea Block and Lighthouse Block, fold quilt top as shown in **Fig. 7**, pin raw edges, and sew from dot to bottom edge (indicated in pink) to make **Quilt Top Center**.

Fig. 7

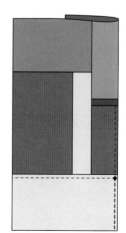

Adding The Borders

1. Matching centers and corners, sew side then top/bottom inner borders to quilt top center.
2. Repeat Step 1 to sew outer borders to quilt top center to complete **Quilt Top**.

COMPLETING THE QUILT

1. Follow **Quilting**, page 117, to mark, layer, and quilt as desired. Our quilt is machine quilted with outline quilting around each appliqué and free-motion detail quilting on the appliqués. There is a wave pattern in the borders.

2. Follow **Making Straight-Grain Binding**, page 121, and **Attaching Binding With Mitered Corners**, page 122, to bind quilt using **binding strips**.

Quilt Top Diagram

Jean's Deviled Crab

Growing up, I would spend hours crabbing off the docks and bridges around my home catching bucketfuls of blue crabs. My mother and I would cook and clean the crabs and use the meat for making Deviled Crab.

- 1 bell pepper
- 4 sprigs celery
- 1 onion

Chop pepper, celery, and onion very fine; sauté in butter.

- 3 slices of very dry rye bread

Soak bread in a small amount of water; squeeze out excess water.

Mix all ingredients with:

- 1 lb crabmeat
- 1 egg
- Worcestershire sauce, hot sauce, and salt to taste

Pack into clean crab shells or individual baking dishes. Sprinkle with paprika. Bake 350°– 400° for 20 minutes.

A

B

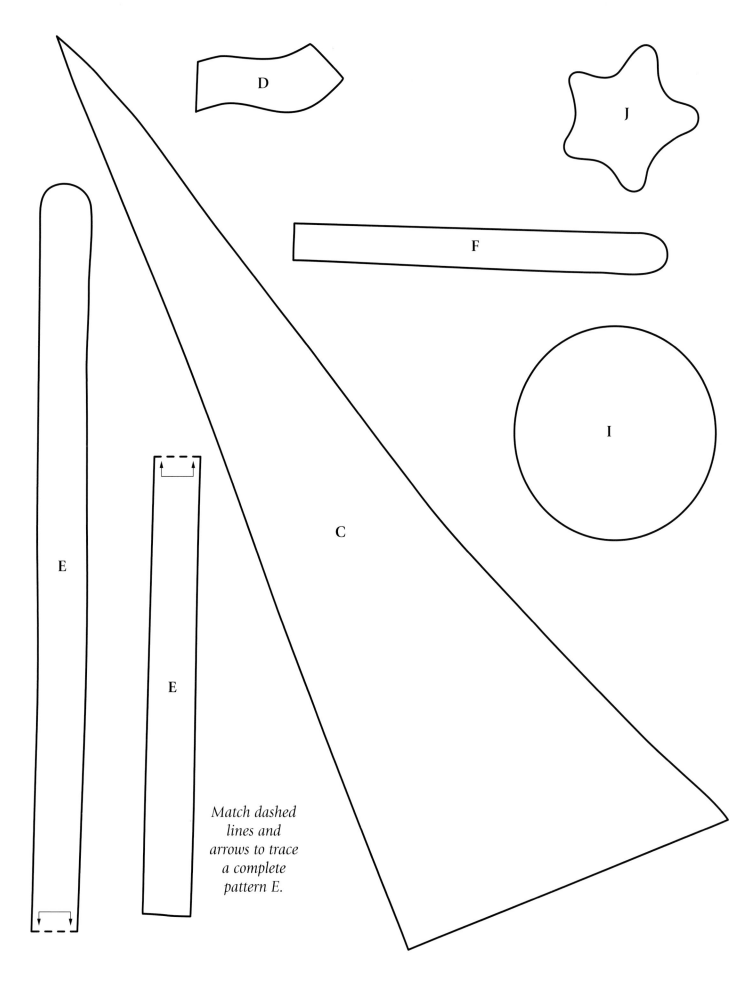

D

J

F

I

C

E

E

*Match dashed
lines and
arrows to trace
a complete
pattern E.*

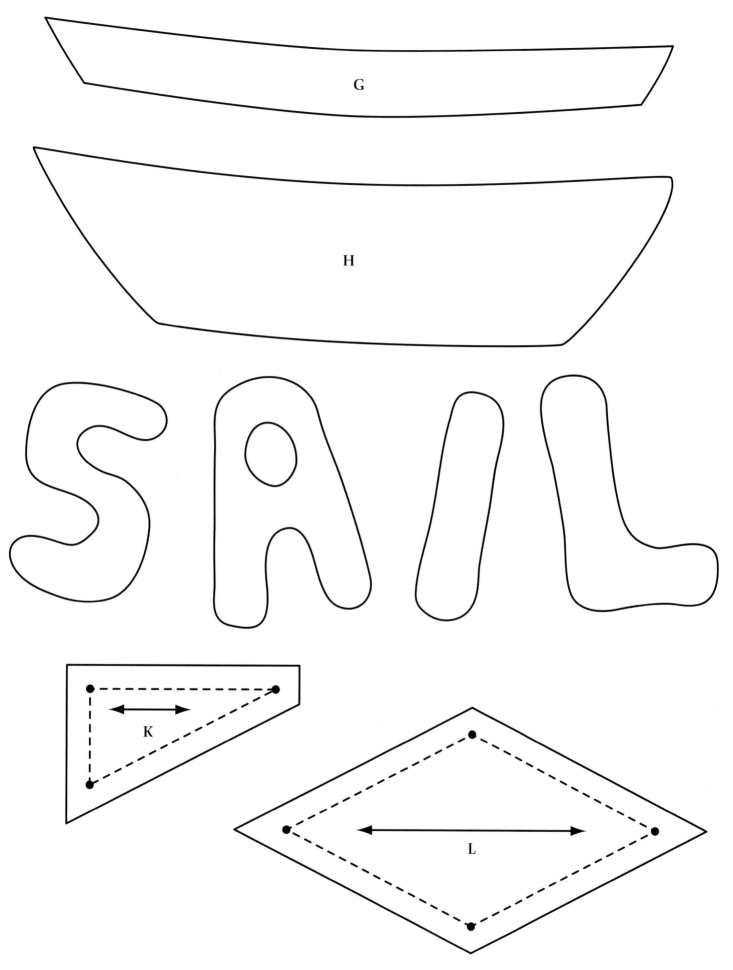

G

H

K

L

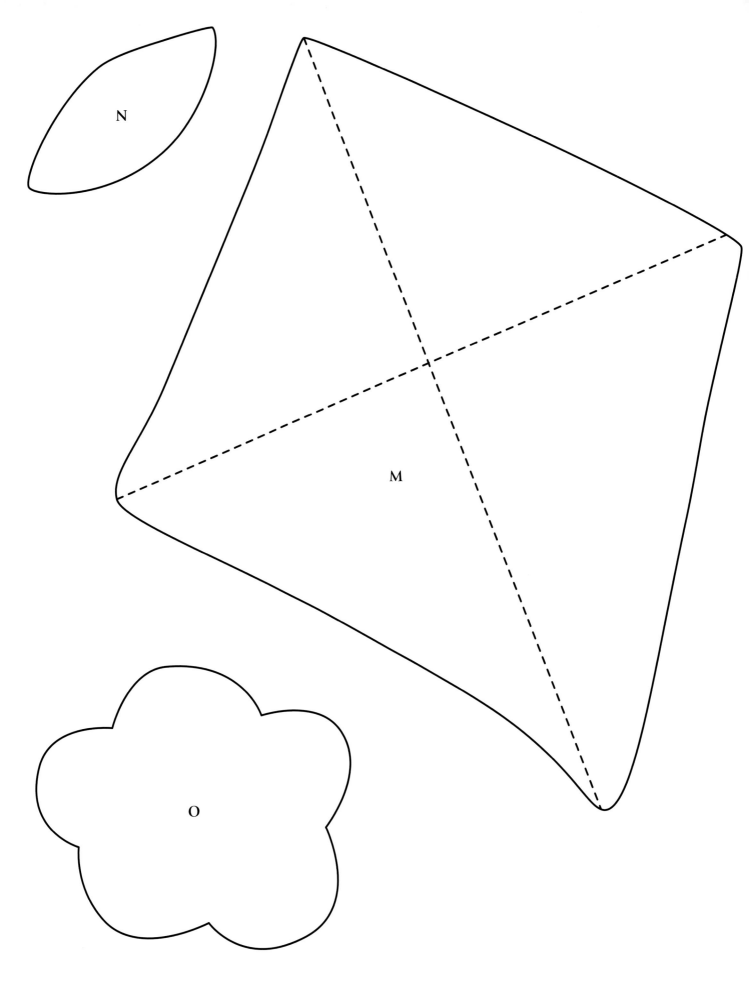

N

M

O

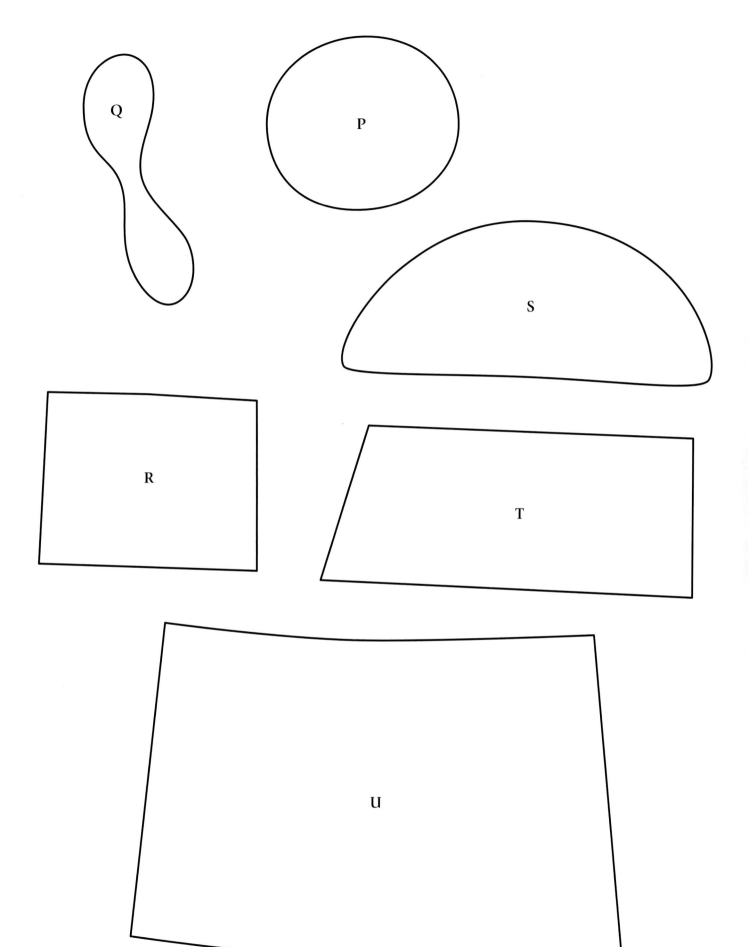

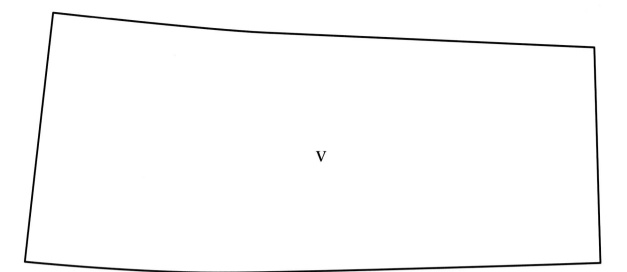

v

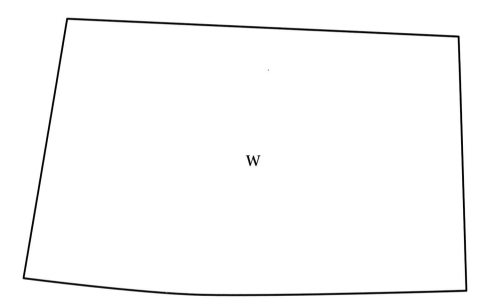

w

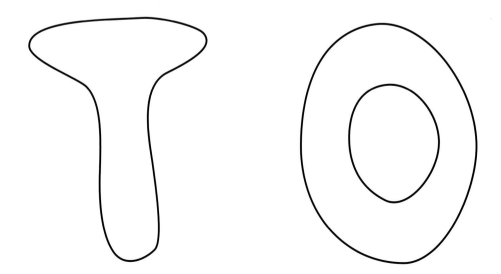

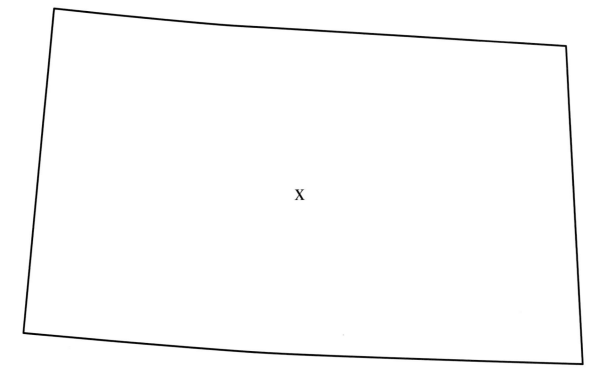

X

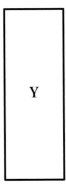

Y

Z

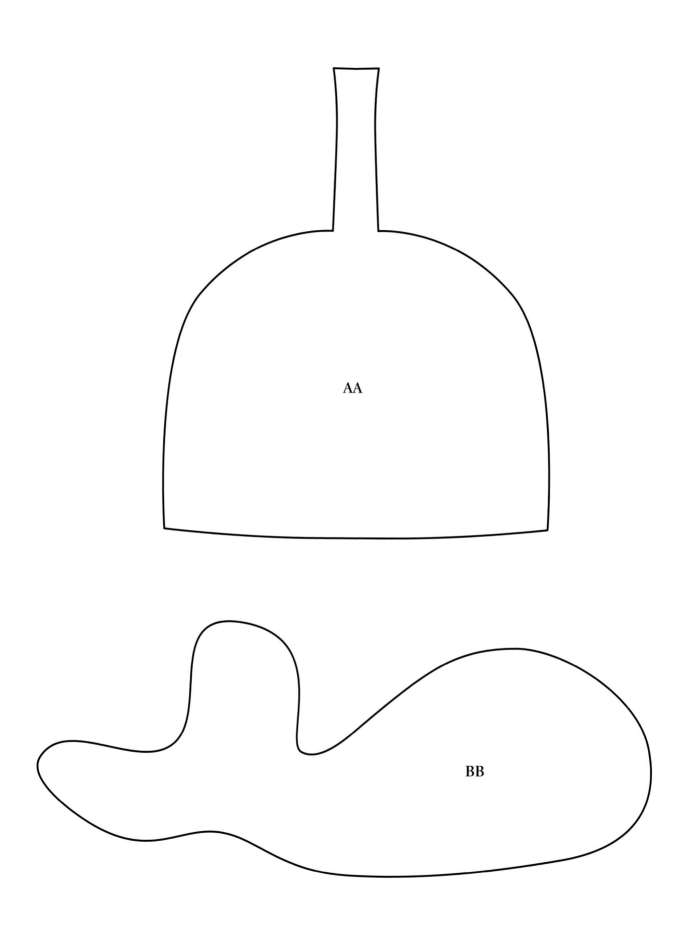

AA

BB

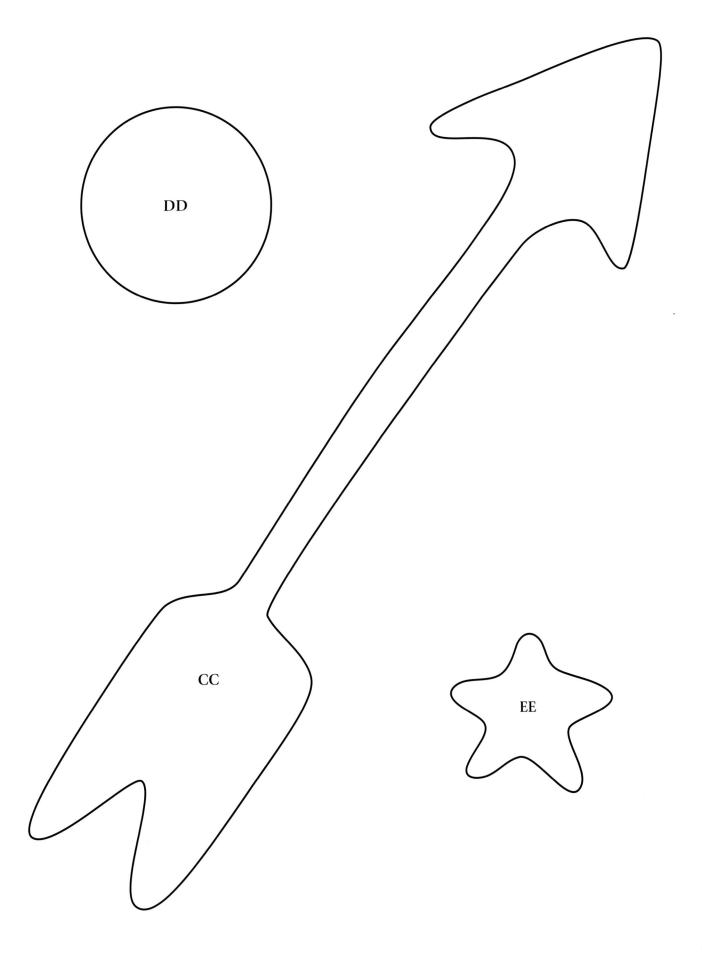

DD

CC

EE

Dear Grid Group,

My Grandma Waldoch loved to crochet — every one of my cousins [there were 55 of us!] received a set of doilies from her as a wedding gift. She had doilies set aside and wrapped so those of us who married after she died still got a set!

There were always boy cousins in and out of Grandma's house, helping with chores. Grandma kept those boys stuffed with homemade cookies, cakes and pies. She baked and cooked on a wood stove and refused to upgrade it when she had the chance. And her hands were always busy — peeling apples, snapping beans, or shelling peas. She washed cucumbers for pickles in her wringer washer!

We celebrated Grandma's 70th wedding anniversary with a huge party — everyone was there, crammed into their house. Grandma sat in her chair and "received" everyone. She went to bed that night and died in her sleep. She loved Grandpa a lot, but we all joked "70 years with that man and not a minute more." Grandpa lived another ten years without her and died at 100 years and six months. He missed her so much. We all did and still do.

Roseann

MEMORIES of GRANDMA

Owner: **Roseann Kermes**
Machine quilted by: **Patti Trygg**

Finished Quilt Size: 33" x 41" (84 cm x 104 cm)

MAKING THE BLOCKS

GENTLE HANDS BLOCK

Finished Block Size: 8" x 16" (20 cm x 41 cm)
Made by: Roseann

I designed my block to resemble a crock, filled with yarn balls, sitting on an oilcloth-covered table in my Grandma's kitchen. The heart and hand appliqués on the crock represent the sentiment that always reminds me of Grandma — gentle hands and a kind heart.

— Roseann

Yardage Requirements

$8^1/_2$" x $10^1/_2$" (22 cm x 27 cm) rectangle of tan fabric (background)

13" x $3^1/_2$" (33 cm x 9 cm) rectangle **each** of 1 cream and 1 red print fabric (pinwheels)

$8^1/_2$" x $2^1/_2$" (22 cm x 6 cm) rectangle of red stripe fabric (background)

7" x 7" (18 cm x 18 cm) square of green wool (crock)

Assorted wool scraps (appliqués)

You will also need:

Template plastic

Red and assorted colors of embroidery floss to match appliqués

Cutting Out The Pieces

Note: When cutting out appliqué pieces A – L, do not add seam allowances.

From *each* cream and red print fabric:
- Cut 4 squares $2^7/_8$" x $2^7/_8$".

From green wool:
- Cut 1 crock (**A**).

From assorted wool scraps:
- Cut 1 crock rim (**B**).
- Cut 1 crock handle (**C**). Cut 1 crock handle reversed (**Cr**).
- Cut 1 hand (**D**).
- Cut 1 heart (**E**).
- Cut 1 of each yarn ball (**F - L**).

Assembling The Block

Use 2 strands of floss for all embroidery.

1. Use floss to match each appliqué and work in alphabetical order to **Straight Stitch** pieces **A – L** to tan background rectangle.

2. Use red floss to make a **Running Stitch** outline around piece **D** to make **Unit 1**.

Unit 1

3. Draw a diagonal line on wrong side of each cream print square. With right sides together, place 1 cream print square on top of 1 red print square. Stitch ¹/₄" from each side of drawn line (**Fig. 1**).

Fig. 1

2. Cut along drawn line. Open up and press to make 2 **Triangle Squares**. Make 8 Triangle-Squares.

Triangle-Squares (make 8)

3. Sew 8 Triangle-Squares together to make **Unit 2**.

Unit 2

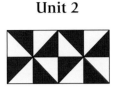

4. Sew Units 1, 2, and red stripe background rectangle together to complete **Gentle Hands Block**.

Gentle Hands Block

GINGERBREAD MEN BLOCK

Finished Block Size: 12" x 12" (30 cm x 30 cm)
Made by: Margi

Dear Roseann,

I had so much fun working with your grid and enjoying all the fun "quilty" stuff you included with your project!

I knew as soon as I read about your grandmother that I wanted to do a block that represented my Grams. When I think of Grams, I can almost smell the gingerbread cookies baking. To represent one of the most wonderful women in my life, I used Pat's Sweet Treats pattern from Quilt the Seasons. I love stars so I had to be sure to include at least one in the block. I'm so glad you included wool in your kit as I've had very few opportunities to work with this medium. I love the dimension it added to the block!

Enjoy and happy quilting!
Margi

Yardage Requirements

12$\frac{1}{2}$" x 12$\frac{1}{2}$" (32 cm x 32 cm) square
of tan print fabric (background)
Assorted scrap fabrics (appliqués)
Assorted wool scraps (appliqués)
You will also need:
Template plastic
Gold, black, and white embroidery floss

Cutting Out The Pieces

*Note: When cutting out appliqué pieces **R – S**, do not add seam allowances.*

From assorted scrap fabrics:
- Cut 2 gingerbread men (**M**).
- Cut 1 bowl (**N**).
- Cut 1 bowl glaze (**O**).
- Cut 1 bowl rim (**P**).
- Cut 1 bowl base (**Q**).

From assorted wool scraps:
- Cut 1 star (**R**).
- Cut 2 scarves (**S**).

Assembling The Block

Use 2 strands of floss for all embroidery.

1. Work in alphabetical order to **Needle-Turn Appliqué** pieces **M – Q** to background.
2. Stitch piece **R** to background using gold floss and a **Running Stitch**.
3. Use black floss to **Blanket Stitch** 1 piece **S** on each gingerbread man. Use white floss to make **French Knot** eyes on the gingerbread men to complete **Gingerbread Men Block**.

Gingerbread Men Block

GRANDMA BLOCK
Finished Block Size: 16" x 8" (41 cm x 20 cm)
Made by: Pat

Roseann, it was a wonderful trip down memory lane reading your thoughts. I had two wonderful grandmothers, Na-na and Granny.

The best part of working on your quilt was picking the thing I wanted to do. I knew as soon as I read your journal that I would add a block representing my grandma. Then one morning, I woke up from a dream and realized cupcakes were the choice (m-m-m — don't know why!)

I searched for those little heart buttons, since I think all grandmas sprinkle love on their cupcakes.

Hugs,
Pat

Yardage Requirements
Two 5$^1/_2$" x 8$^1/_2$" (14 cm x 22 cm) rectangles of blue plaid fabric (background)
6$^1/_2$" x 8$^1/_2$" (17 cm x 22 cm) rectangle of blue stripe fabric (background)
Assorted scrap fabrics (appliqués)
7" x 8" (18 cm x 20 cm) rectangle of brown wool (letters)
You will also need:
Template plastic
3 novelty buttons
Tan No. 5 pearl cotton

Cutting Out The Pieces
Note: When cutting out appliqué pieces GRANDMA, do not add seam allowances.
From assorted scrap fabrics:
- Cut 3 cupcakes (**T**) from like fabric.
- Cut 3 icings (**U**).

From brown wool:
- Cut the letters to spell **GRANDMA**.

Assembling The Block
1. Sew the 3 background rectangles together to make **block background**.
2. Work in alphabetical order to **Needle-Turn Appliqué** pieces **T** - **U** to block background.
3. Use pearl cotton to **Blanket Stitch** the letters **GRANDMA** to block background.
4. Sew 1 button to the top of each cupcake to complete **Grandma Block**.

Grandma Block

SEWING MACHINE BLOCK

Finished Block Size: 16" x 8" (41 cm x 20 cm)
Made by: Jean

Yardage Requirements

16¹/₂" x 5" (42 cm x 13 cm) rectangle of red stripe fabric (background)

16¹/₂" x 4" (42 cm x 10 cm) rectangle of brown print fabric (background)

12" x 10" (30 cm x 25 cm) rectangle of black print fabric (sewing machine)

Assorted scrap fabrics (appliqués)

Assorted scraps of wool (appliqués)

You will also need:

Template plastic

Assorted buttons

7 (3mm) dia. round pearl beads

³/₈ yd (34 cm) of ¹/₂" (13 mm) wide tape measure ribbon

Tan, green, gold, and grey embroidery floss

Red No. 3 pearl cotton

Cutting Out The Pieces

Note: When cutting out appliqué pieces FF–II, do not add seam allowances.

From assorted scrap fabrics:
- Cut a **total** of 7 strips $5^1/4$" long that vary in width from 1"-$1^1/2$" (**V**).
- Cut 1 sewing machine base (**W**).
- Cut 1 throat plate (**Y**).
- Cut 1 needle shaft (**Z**).
- Cut 1 balance wheel trim (**AA**).
- Cut 1 face plate (**CC**).
- Cut 1 tape measure end (**DD**).
- Cut 1 thread (**EE**).

From black print fabric:
- Cut 1 sewing machine head (**BB**).
- Cut 1 sewing machine bed (**X**).

From assorted scraps of wool:
- Cut 1 spool (**FF**).
- Cut 1 pincushion (**GG**).
- Cut 1 pincushion top (**HH**).
- Cut 1 oval trim (**II**).

Assembling The Block

Use 2 strands of floss for all embroidery.

1. Sew red stripe and brown background rectangles together to make **block background**.
2. Matching long edges, sew 7 assorted scrap fabric strips together to make piece **V**. Trim side edges of **V** to make each fabric strip have a slightly curved edge. Working in alphabetical order, **Needle-Turn Appliqué** pieces **V - Z** to block background.
3. Appliqué long edges of piece **AA** to piece **BB**. Appliqué right edge of piece **CC** to piece **BB**.
4. Leaving an approximately $3/4$" wide opening in center top and in lower right side of piece **BB**, for inserting ribbon, appliqué piece **BB** to block background.
5. Insert ribbon through openings in piece **BB**, position and then **Blindstitch** openings closed. Fold under raw edge of ribbon on right side of piece **BB**. Blindstitch across folded end and along top edge of ribbon for approximately 1". Appliqué piece **DD** over remaining raw end of ribbon.
6. Appliqué top and bottom edges of piece **EE** to piece **FF**. Appliqué sides of piece **FF** to background rectangle. Use tan floss to **Straight Stitch** top and bottom edges of piece **FF** to block background.
7. Use pearl cotton to **Blanket Stitch** piece **GG** to block background. Use green floss to **Straight Stitch** piece **HH** to piece **GG**. Use green floss to **Couch** detail lines on piece **GG**. Use grey floss to make **Straight Stitch** "pins" topped with pearl beads.
8. Use gold floss to appliqué piece **II** to sewing machine with **Straight Stitches** and grey floss to **Stem Stitch** sewing machine details.
9. Sew buttons to block background to complete **Sewing Machine Block**.

Sewing Machine Block

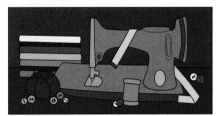

COFFEEPOT BLOCK

Finished Block Size: 12" x 16" (30 cm x 41 cm)
Made by: Sandee

Dear Roseann,

My Grandma Storm was number 13 of 14 children. She was raised on a farm, and when she married my grandfather, they farmed together. We lived one farm apart from my grandparents. With everyone involved in farming, lots of family meetings revolved around my grandmother's kitchen table. When I heard my mother say "We're going to Grandma's for coffee," I knew there would be a lot of adult talk about farming. I remember Grandma's large blue coffeepot with white trim, so I made that as my block for your quilt.

My grandmother worked hard as a farmer's wife. Her kitchen was always full of the smells of cooking and baking. She raised chickens and sold the eggs for mad money. She did embroidery and made quilts which she tied. Once, when I asked her if she ever hand quilted any, she said "No. I never had time for that. It was more important to get the quilts on the beds so we didn't freeze to death in the winter."

She was a grand lady.

Sandee

Yardage Requirements

One 7¹/₂" x 18¹/₂" (19 cm x 47 cm) rectangle **each** of cream print and green check fabrics (strip set)

7" x 13" (18 cm x 33 cm) rectangle of brown print fabric (borders)

12¹/₂" x 4³/₈" (32 cm x 11 cm) rectangle of red print fabric (table)

9" x 10" (23 cm x 25 cm) rectangle of blue wool (coffeepot)

You will also need:

Template plastic
Black and red embroidery floss
10" (25 cm) of heavy lace trim
1 linen and lace 8" (20 cm) dia. doily

Cutting Out The Pieces

Note: When cutting out appliqué pieces JJ–KK, do not add seam allowances.

From *each* cream print and green check fabric:
- Cut 5 strips 1³/₈" x 18".

From brown print fabric:
- Cut 2 side borders 2¹/₈" x 11".
- Cut 1 top border 2¹/₈" x 12¹/₂".

From blue wool:
- Cut 1 coffeepot (**JJ**).
- Cut 1 coffeepot knob (**KK**).

Assembling The Block

Use 2 strands of floss for all embroidery.

1. Alternating colors, sew cream and green strips together to make **Strip Set**. Cut across Strip Set at 1³/₈" intervals to make **Unit 1**. Make 12 Unit 1's.

Strip Set   **Unit 1** (make 12)

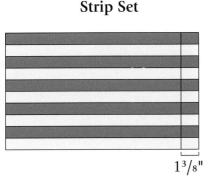

1³/₈"

2. Alternating direction, sew Unit 1's into Rows to make **block background**.

Block Background

3. Sew side and then top borders to block background.
4. On wrong side, lightly draw a line through center of doily. Trim along drawn line. Center raw edge of doily on bottom edge of block background; pin. Matching right sides and raw edges, sew red print rectangle to block background and doily; press open.
5. Use black floss to **Blanket Stitch** pieces **JJ** and **KK** to block background.
6. Cut 2 pieces of lace, one 3¹/₂" and one 5¹/₂" long. Turning under raw edges on each end, hand stitch lace to piece **JJ**.
7. Use red floss to make a **Running Stitch** heart in center of **JJ** to complete **Coffeepot Block**.

Coffeepot Block

HEART BLOCK

Finished Block Size: 12" x 4" (30 cm x 10 cm)
Made by: Roseann

Yardage Requirements

$5^1/_2$" x 16" (14 cm x 41 cm) rectangle of black
print fabric (background)
Assorted scrap fabrics (flying geese)
Assorted scraps of wool (heart and flower)
You will also need:
Template plastic
Black and gold embroidery floss

Cutting Out The Pieces

*Note: When cutting out appliqué pieces do not add
seam allowances.*

From black print fabric:
- Cut 1 large square $4^1/_2$" x $4^1/_2$".
- Cut 8 small squares $2^1/_2$" x $2^1/_2$".

From assorted scrap fabrics:
- Cut 4 rectangles $4^1/_2$" x $2^1/_2$".

From assorted scraps of wool:
- Cut 1 heart (**LL**).
- Cut 1 flower (**MM**).
- Cut 1 flower center (**NN**).

Assembling The Block

1. Place 1 small square on 1 corner of 1 rectangle
   and stitch diagonally (**Fig. 2**). Trim $^1/_4$" from
   stitching line (**Fig. 3**). Open up and press seam
   allowance toward darker fabric (**Fig. 4**).

Fig. 2   **Fig. 3**   **Fig. 4**

2. Place another small square on opposite corner
   of rectangle. Stitch, trim, and press as in Step 1
   to make 1 **Flying Geese Unit**. Make 4 Flying
   Geese Units.

Flying Geese Unit (make 4)

3. Sew large square and 4 Flying Geese Units
   together to make **block center**.
4. Using black floss, **Straight Stitch** piece **LL** to
   background rectangle. Place piece **MM**, topped
   with piece **NN**, on center of piece **LL**. **Straight
   Stitch** around edges of piece **NN** with gold
   floss to complete **Heart Block**.

Heart Block

When my quilt came home there was a "hole" to fill
between Jean's and Margi's blocks. I made a block
using four flying geese units and a plain center
square. I appliqued a pineapple in the center
square. However, before I sewed all the blocks
together, I decided to change the pineapple to
a heart. I feel the heart expresses my theme
better.

— Roseann

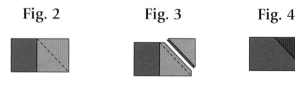

98

MAKING THE QUILT TOP

Borders
Yardage Requirements

$^1/_4$ yd (23 cm) of black solid fabric
  (inner border)
$^1/_4$ yd (23 cm) of red print fabric
  (outer border)
1 fat quarter* **each** of 1 black and
  1 tan print fabric (triangle-squares)
20" x 20" (51 cm x 51 cm) square
  of black stripe fabric (binding)
$2^3/_4$ yds (2.5 m) of backing fabric

You will also need:
  41" x 49" (104 cm x 124 cm) rectangle
    of batting

  *Fat quarter = approximately 18" x 22"
    (46 cm x 56 cm)

Cutting Out The Pieces

From black solid fabric:
- Cut 2 inner top/bottom borders
  $1^1/_4$" x 26".
- Cut 2 inner side borders $1^1/_4$" x $32^1/_2$".

From red print fabric:
- Cut 1 outer top border 3" x $28^1/_2$".
- Cut 1 outer side border 3" x 34".

From *each* fat quarter:
- Cut 3 strips $4^7/_8$" x 22". From these strips,
  cut 9 squares $4^7/_8$" x $4^7/_8$".

Assembling The Quilt Top Center

*Refer to **Quilt Top Diagram**, page 100, for placement.*
1. Sew Gingerbread Men, Heart, and Coffeepot Blocks together to make **Unit 1**.
2. Sew Sewing Machine, Grandma, and Gentle Hands Blocks together to make **Unit 2**.
3. Sew Units 1 and 2 together to make **Quilt Top Center**.

Adding The Borders

1. Matching centers and corners, sew side then top/bottom inner borders to quilt top center.
2. Draw a diagonal line on wrong side of each tan print square. With right sides together, place 1 tan print square on top of 1 black print square. Stitch $^1/_4$" from each side of drawn line (**Fig. 5**).

Fig. 5

3. Cut along drawn line. Open up and press to make 2 **Triangle-Squares**. Make 18 Triangle-Squares. *Note:* You will only use 17 Triangle-Squares.

Triangle-Squares (make 18)

4. Sew 9 Triangle-Squares together to make **left side border**. Sew 8 Triangle-Squares together to make **bottom border**.
5. Matching centers and corners, sew right side, top, left side and bottom borders to quilt top center to complete **Quilt Top**.

COMPLETING THE QUILT

1. Follow **Quilting**, page 117, to mark, layer, and quilt as desired. Our quilt is machine quilted with outline quilting around each appliqué. There are free-motion leaves, swirls, waves, and feathers quilted in the **block backgrounds**. There is a continuous star pattern in the solid borders and feathers in the pieced borders.
2. Use binding square and follow **Making Continuous Bias Binding**, page 120, to make 2¹/₄" wide binding. Follow **Attaching Binding With Mitered Corners**, page122, to bind quilt.

Roseann's Gumdrop Fruitcake

Grandma started making this when she got tired of us picking the expensive (but yucky) fruit out of her fruitcake. We liked this much better! When I was serving in the Army, she would send me one in a care package. Mix the following in a pot and bring to a boil.

- 2 cups white sugar
- 1 tsp cinnamon
- 1 tsp nutmeg
- ½ tsp cloves
- 1lb bag of spicy miniature gumdrops (no licorice)
- 2 cups liquid — part water and part cherry juice
- 2 cups raisins

Cool and then add the following:

- 1 cup shortening — part should be butter
- 1 large jar maraschino cherries
- 2 eggs
- 3¹/₂ cups flour
- 2 tsp baking soda
- 1 tsp salt
- 1¹/₂ cups chopped walnuts

Mix well and pour into 4 medium-size loaf pans. Bake in a slow oven (300° – 325°) for about 1 hour and 15 minutes, or until top springs back when touched. Freezes well.

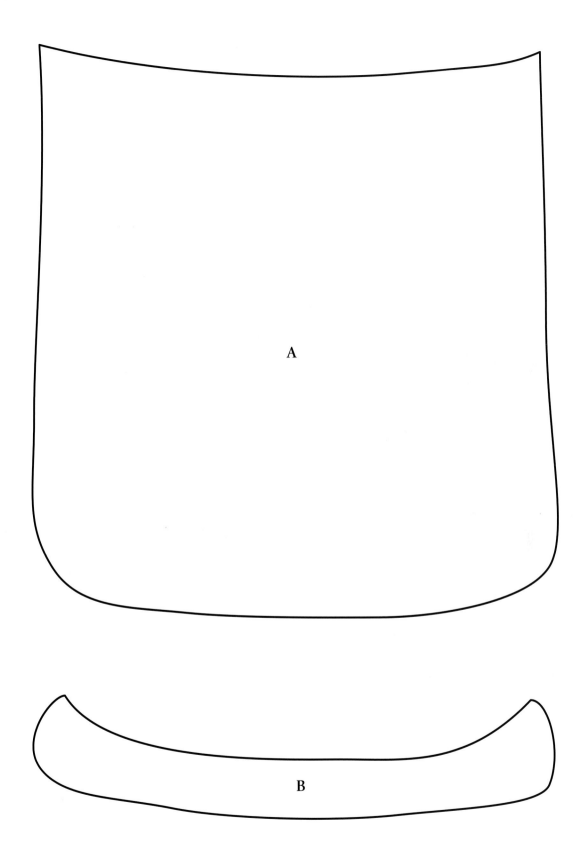

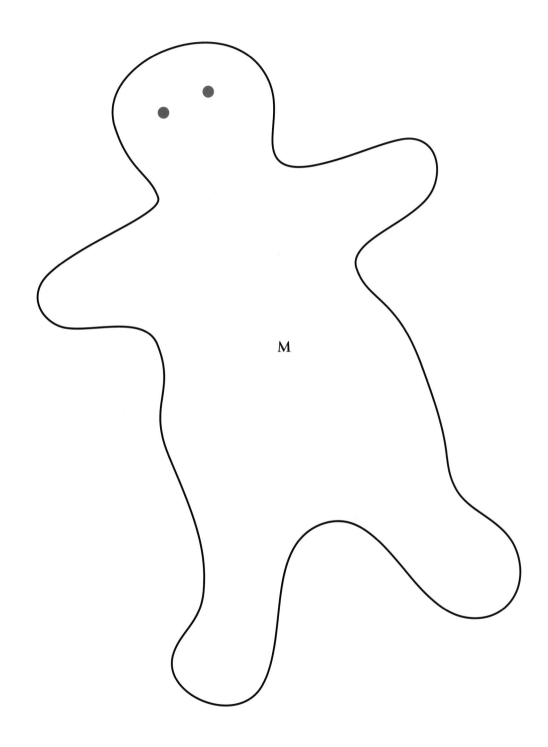

M

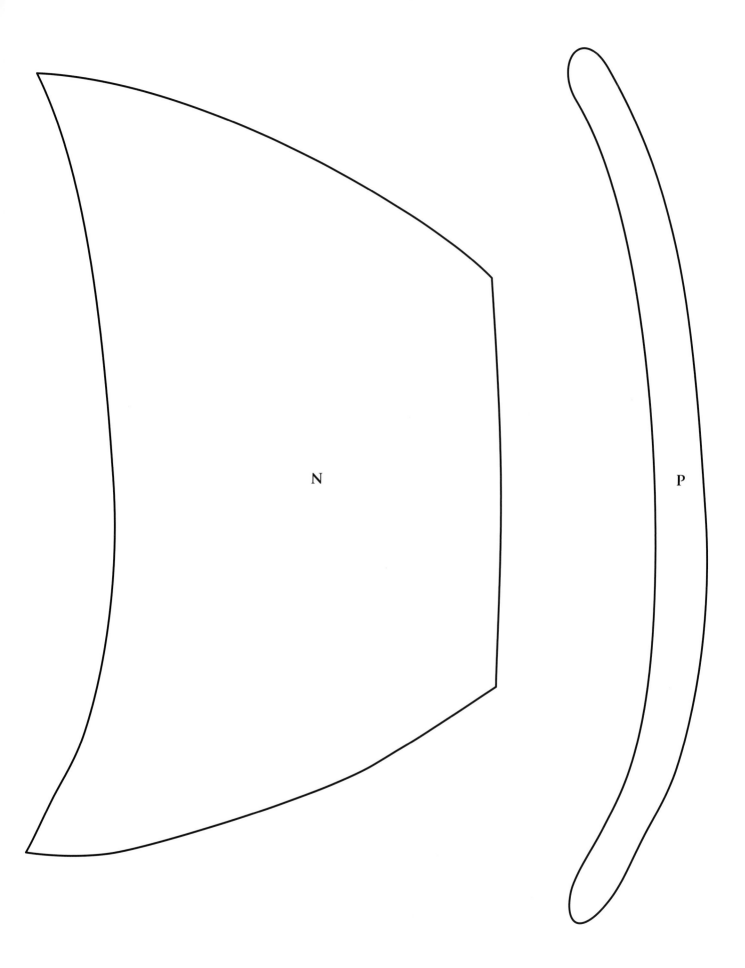

N

P

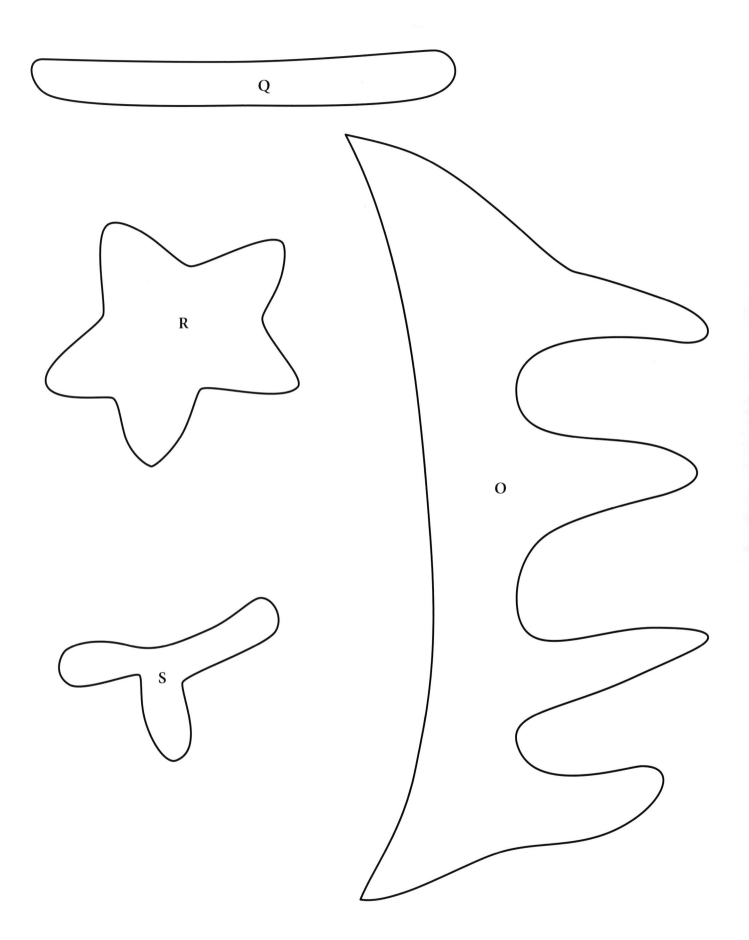

Q

R

S

O

T

U

G R A

N D M

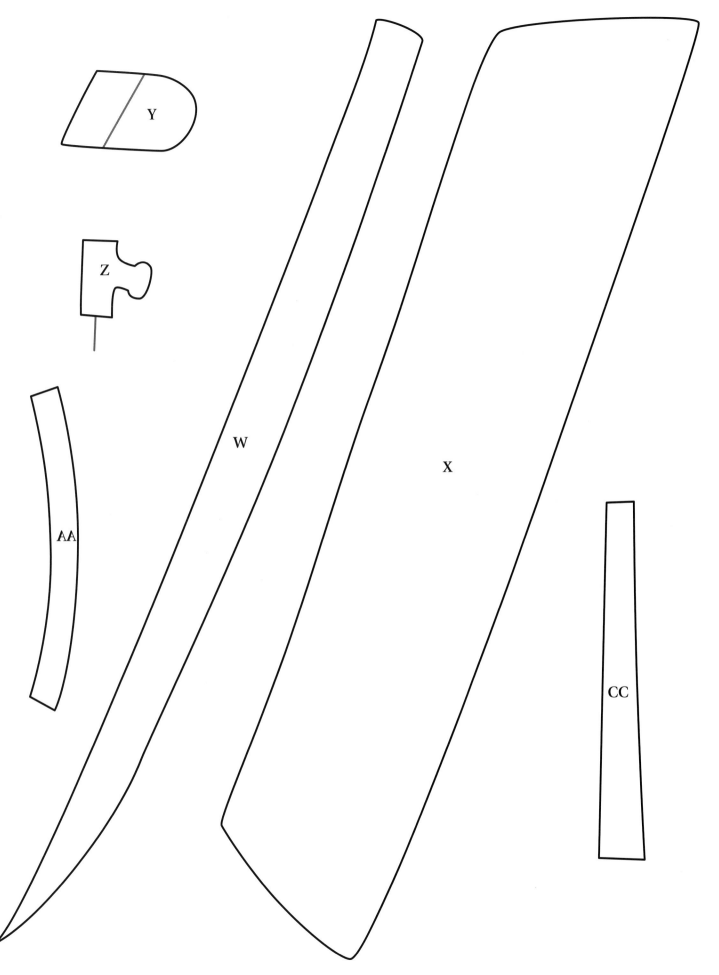

Y

Z

W

X

AA

CC

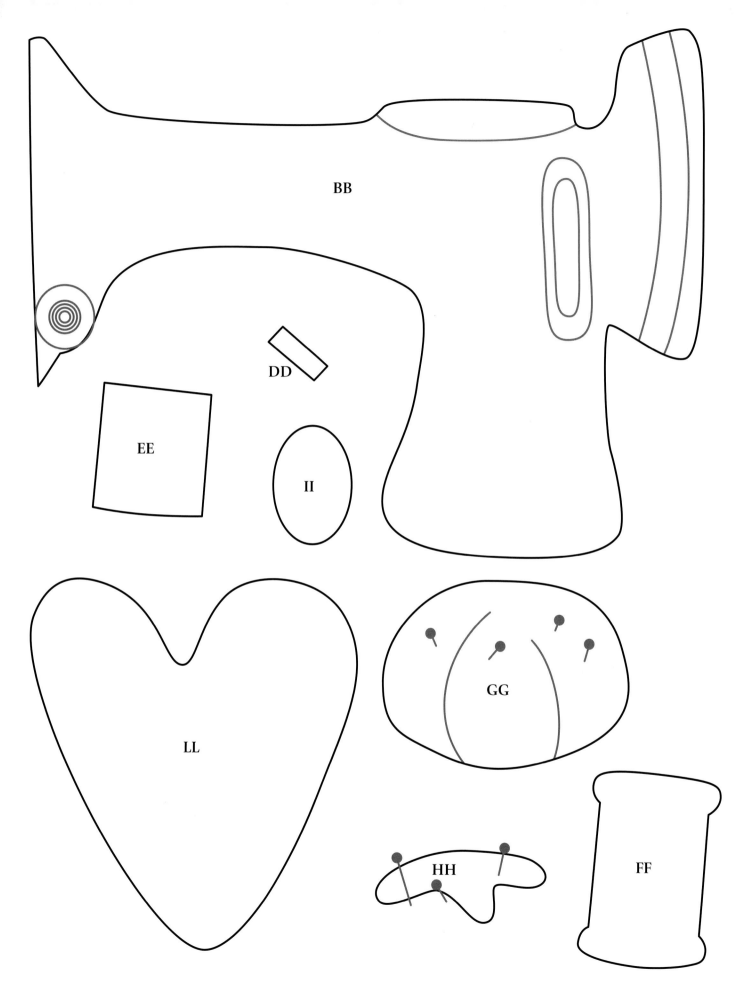

MM

NN

KK

JJ

All I can say is WOW!

We were ALL blown away by the detail and workmanship on these beautiful quilts, by the love and caring that went into each one, and by the everlasting friendship these quilts brought us. On pages 111 - 113, you will find my Tips For The Organizer and Participants of a Block By Block round robin. My hope is that your group will have a highly successful round robin, too!

— Pat

I'm sad the project is over, but I look forward to seeing the finished book. I'm thankful for my new friends, Jean, Margi, and Roseann, and especially for my friend Pat for including me in this fun project.
Thanks!
Sandee

I think getting to know you guys was a huge bonus to my participation. I feel like you are my pals...like you live right here in town. It's been fun! Thanks for including me, Pat! Can we play again?

— Roseann

Tips For The Organizer/Host

1. **Encourage Communication-** I *truly believe* that if communication is strong your round robin will be totally successful. Chat with the members frequently, encourage them to keep in touch with each other, and keep everyone informed about the status of the projects.

2. **Provide Clear Rules and Guidelines** - The Rules and Guidelines in this book have been revised and fine-tuned and should answer most questions that arise. Feel free to use them as is or adapt them as needed for your group.

3. **Group Members By Experience Levels** - New quilters worry about their inexperience. If the group is *all* new quilters, they will relax and have fun. Advanced quilters tend to use complex techniques and a lot of detail. Intermediate quilters can usually go with the flow of either group.

4. **Establish A Short Turn Around-Time -** A turn-around time of about 4 weeks is the best. Most people will only begin working on the project a few days before it's due to be passed along — really!

5. **If Someone Can't Meet A Deadline -** Have her pass the project on to the next person. Sometimes "Life Happens" – find out if they need to drop out or just need to have some "time off." If they want to continue, have them make their block at the end of the rotation. Remind everyone this is for FUN so they should not get stressed over deadlines.

Tips For The Participant

1. **Check your schedule** - There are firm dates when the projects must be passed to the next person. Before you sign up, look at your personal schedule. Can you meet the dates? Be sure to allow 3 to 5 days for mailing and to act as a buffer if problems arise.

2. **If You Can't Meet A Deadline** - If "Life Happens" and you just can't work on a block, inform your organizer and she will help you work out a solution. Don't let several projects pile up at your house.

3. **Enjoy Your Time To Play!** - I feel that being in a round robin is my time to "Play." Because most of the blocks are small you can try new techniques without having to make a large project. Remember all those reasons you joined!

4. **Read The Rules And Guidelines** - They will contain all the information you need to know about your Block-By-Block round robin.

5. **Relax And "Let Go"** - We should all relax and have fun working on the quilts. The members of your group will treat your quilt with love and affection and it will return with stories to be told, fabric to be touched, and techniques to be admired.

6. **Provide Clear Theme Guidelines** - I find the most successful quilts have a theme. It can be anything from "A day at the beach" to "pink and brown pieced baskets." The clearer you are about the theme, the better. Include in your package any items that might help the group follow your theme.

7. **Respect Other Members' Themes** - Years ago when I did a round robin, I specified that I wanted an angel. When my quilt reached the last person, she noticed that no one before her had included an angel, so she knew right away what she was adding!

8. **Keep The Keepsakes At Home** - I highly recommend that you NEVER attach a sentimental item to a quilt while it is being passed around. Mail can get lost and things do fall out of packages. Keep grandmother's block or mom's hankie at home and add it at the end. You could send a photo of the item and a note about its placement on your starter block. Better safe than sorry.

9. **Common Fears** - Many people tell me they have never tried a round robin because they are afraid to work on someone else's quilt. They are afraid they might not do a good job, the person might be disappointed, or that they themselves might be disappointed in their own quilt.

First - Other people in the group are usually a bit anxious, too, if they have never done this before. But all of you decided to play so you know that the other members expect and want you to work on their piece. It's okay!

Second - I feel in order to grow and learn new things we have to take a risk. Working on quilts designed by someone else will really expand your thinking. Everyone who has done a Block-By-Block round robin tells me they are so glad they did!

Third - Will you like what comes back to you? Usually you will more than like it, you will be overwhelmed with joy! But sometimes a quilt comes back and one block might not quite fit in. Remember, your quilt is not finished when it returns to you! You can change, add, or in the worst case, you can replace a block that is just not working. After all, it's your quilt!

10. **Communication** - Every successful Block-By-Block round robin I've participated in, or hosted, has everyone chatting and getting to know each other. This is the FUN part of the round robin for many quilters. If you communicate with each other, a very successful and a fun Block-By-Block round robin will happen!

Complete instructions are given for making each of the projects shown in this book. To make your project easier and more enjoyable, we encourage you to carefully read all the general instructions, study the color photographs, and familiarize yourself with the individual project instructions before beginning a project.

ROTARY CUTTING

Rotary cutting has brought speed and accuracy to quiltmaking by allowing quilters to easily cut strips of fabric and then cut those strips into smaller pieces.

- Place fabric on work surface with fold closest to you.

- Cut all strips from the selvage-to-selvage width of the fabric unless otherwise indicated in project instructions.

- Square left edge of fabric using rotary cutter and rulers (**Figs. 1 - 2**).

Fig. 1	Fig. 2

- To cut each strip required for a project, place the ruler over the cut edge of the fabric, aligning desired marking on the ruler with the cut edge (**Fig. 3**); make the cut.

Fig. 3

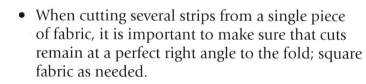

- When cutting several strips from a single piece of fabric, it is important to make sure that cuts remain at a perfect right angle to the fold; square fabric as needed.

TEMPLATE CUTTING

Our piecing template patterns include a $^1/_4$" seam allowance. Patterns for appliqué templates do not include seam allowances. On applique patterns, black solid lines (———) indicate cutting lines, black dashed lines (– – – –) indicate overlaps, and grey solid lines (———) indicate embroidery details. When cutting instructions say to cut in reverse, place the template upside down on the fabric to cut piece in reverse.

1. To make a template from a pattern, use a permanent fine-point pen to carefully trace the pattern onto template plastic, making sure to transfer all markings. Cut out template along outer drawn line. Check template against original pattern for accuracy.

2. To use a piecing template, place template on wrong side of fabric (unless otherwise indicated), aligning grain line on template with straight grain of fabric. Use a sharp fabric marking pencil to draw around template. Cut out fabric piece using scissors or rotary cutting equipment.

3. To use an appliqué template, place template on right side of appliqué fabric. Use a pencil to lightly draw around template, leaving at least $^1/_2$" between shapes; repeat for number of appliqués specified in project instructions. Cut out shapes a scant $^1/_4$" outside drawn line unless otherwise noted in project instructions.

PIECING & PRESSING

Precise cutting, followed by accurate piecing and careful pressing, will ensure that all the pieces of your quilt top fit together well.

PIECING

- Set sewing machine stitch length for approximately 11 stitches per inch.

- Use a neutral-colored general-purpose sewing thread (not quilting thread) in the needle and in the bobbin.

- An accurate $^1/_4$" seam allowance is *essential*. Presser feet that are $^1/_4$" wide are available for most sewing machines.

- When piecing, always place pieces *right sides* together and match raw edges; pin if necessary.

- Chain piecing saves time and will usually result in more accurate piecing.

- Trim away points of seam allowances that extend beyond edges of sewn seams.

Sewing Across Seam Intersections

When sewing across the intersection of two seams, place pieces right sides together and match seams exactly, making sure seam allowances are pressed in opposite directions (**Fig. 4**).

Fig. 4

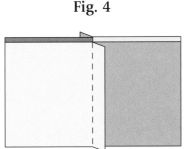

Sewing Strip Sets

When there are several strips to assemble into a strip set, first sew the strips together into pairs, then sew the pairs together to form the strip set. To help avoid distortion, sew 1 seam in 1 direction and then sew the next seam in the opposite direction (**Fig. 5**).

Fig. 5

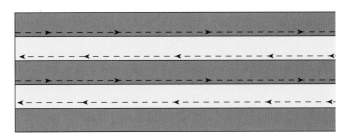

Sewing Sharp Points

To ensure sharp points when joining triangular or diagonal pieces, stitch across the center of the "X" (shown in pink) formed on wrong side by previous seams (**Fig. 6**).

Fig. 6

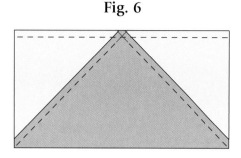

PRESSING

- Use a steam iron set on "Cotton" for all pressing.

- Press after sewing each seam.

- Seam allowances are almost always pressed to one side, usually toward the darker fabric. However, to reduce bulk it may occasionally be necessary to press seam allowances toward the lighter fabric or even to press them open.

- To prevent a dark fabric seam allowance from showing through a light fabric, trim the darker seam allowance slightly narrower than the lighter seam allowance.

- To press long seams, such as those in long strip sets, without curving or other distortion, lay strips across the width of the ironing board.

NEEDLE-TURN APPLIQUÉ

*In this traditional hand appliqué method, the needle is used to turn the seam allowance under as you sew the appliqué to the background fabric using a **Blind Stitch**, page 125 (**Fig. 39**). Stitches on the right side of fabric should not show. Stitches on the edge of an appliqué and on background fabric should be equal in length. It is not necessary to appliqué areas that will be enclosed in a seam.*

1. Clip inside curves and points to, but not through drawn line on appliqué shapes. Arrange shapes on background fabric, as indicated in project instructions, and pin or baste in place.

2. Thread a sharps needle with a single strand of general-purpose sewing thread the color of the appliqué; knot one end.

3. Begin on as straight an edge as possible and use point of needle to turn under a small amount of seam allowance, concealing drawn line on appliqué. Blindstitch appliqué to the background, turning under the seam allowance and stitching to completely secure appliqué.

4. To stitch outward points, stitch to 1/2" from point (**Fig. 7**). Turn seam allowance under at point (**Fig. 8**); then turn remainder of seam allowance between stitching and point. Stitch to point, taking two or three stitches at top of point to secure. Turn under small amount of seam allowance past point and resume stitching.

Fig. 7   **Fig. 8**

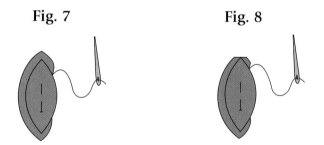

5. To stitch inward point, stitch to 1/2" from point (**Fig. 9**). Clip to but not through seam allowance at point (**Fig. 10**). Turn seam allowance under between stitching and point. Stitch to point, taking two or three stitches at point to secure. Turn under small amount of seam allowance past point and resume stitching.

Fig. 9   **Fig. 10**

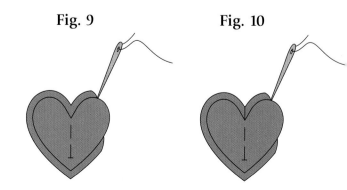

. Do not turn under or stitch seam allowances that will be covered by other appliqué pieces.
. To appliqué pressed bias strips, baste strips in place and blindstitch along edges.

Pat's Outside The Lines Appliqué

For appliqué pieces that flow from one block to another or into the borders, Pat uses her "outside the lines" technique when appliquéing.

. Arrange appliqués on background as they will appear on finished project, allowing pieces that are "outside the lines" to hang off the edges of the background.
. Appliqué pieces that extend off the edge to about 1" from edge. Appliqué all pieces that fit completely on the background.
. Fold back, then pin out of the way any appliqué pieces that hang off the background.
. Sew adjoining section, block, or border to background.
. Un-pin, arrange the appliqués, and finish stitching around these pieces.

QUILTING

Quilting holds the 3 layers (top, batting, and backing) of the quilt together and can be done by hand or machine. Because marking, layering, and quilting are interrelated and may be done in different orders depending on circumstances, please read the entire Quilting section, pages 117 - 119, before beginning project.

TYPES OF QUILTING
In the Ditch Quilting
Quilting along seamlines or along edges of appliquéd pieces is called "in the ditch" quilting. This type of quilting should be done on the side **opposite** the seam allowance and does not need to be marked.

Outline Quilting
Quilting a consistent distance, usually $1/4$", from a seam or appliqué is called "outline" quilting. Outline quilting may be marked, or $1/4$"w masking tape may be placed along seamlines for a quilting guide. (Do not leave tape on quilt longer than necessary, since it may leave an adhesive residue.)

Motif Quilting
Quilting a design, such as a feathered wreath is called "motif" quilting. This type of quilting should be marked before basting quilt layers together.

Echo Quilting
Quilting that follows the outline of an appliquéd or pieced design with 2 or more parallel lines is called "echo" quilting. This type of quilting does not need to be marked.

Meandering Quilting
Quilting in random curved lines and swirls is called "meandering" quilting. Quilting lines should not cross or touch each other. This type of quilting does not need to be marked.

MARKING QUILTING LINES
Quilting lines may be marked using fabric marking pencils, chalk markers, water-or air-soluble pens, or lead pencils.

Simple quilting designs may be marked with chalk or chalk pencil after basting. A small area may be marked, then quilted, before moving to next area to be marked. Intricate designs should be marked before basting using a more durable marker.

Caution: Pressing may permanently set some marks. Test different markers **on scrap fabric** to find one that marks clearly and can be thoroughly removed.

A wide variety of precut quilting stencils, as well as entire books of quilting patterns, are available. Using a stencil makes it easier to mark intricate or repetitive designs on your quilt top.

To make a stencil from a pattern, center template plastic over pattern and use a permanent marker to trace pattern onto plastic. Use a craft knife with a single or double blade to cut narrow slits along traced lines (**Fig. 11**). Use desired marking tool and stencil to mark quilting lines.

Fig. 11

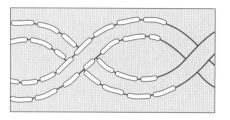

PREPARING THE BACKING
To allow for slight shifting of quilt top during quilting, backing should be approximately 4" larger on all sides. Yardage requirements listed for quilt backings are calculated for 43"/44"w fabric. To piece a backing using 43"/44"w fabric, use the following instructions.

1. Measure length and width of quilt top; add 8" to each measurement.
2. If determined width is 79" or less, cut backing fabric into two lengths slightly longer than determined **length** measurement. Trim selvages. Place lengths with right sides facing and sew long edges together, forming tube (**Fig. 12**). Match seams and press along one fold (**Fig. 13**). Cut along pressed fold to form single piece (**Fig. 14**).

| **Fig. 12** | **Fig. 13** | **Fig. 14** |

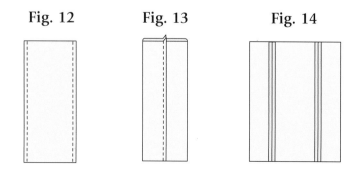

3. Trim backing to size determined in Step 1; pres seam allowances open.

CHOOSING AND PREPARING THE BATTING
Choosing the right batting will make your quilting job easier. The projects in this book are made using cotton batting which does not require tight quilting. If machine quilting, choose a low-loft all cotton or a cotton/polyester blend batting because the cotton helps "grip" the layers of the quilt. For hand quilting, choose a low-loft batting in any of the fiber types described here.

Batting options include cotton/polyester batting, which combines the best of both polyester and cotton battings; fusible battings which do not need to be basted before quilting; bonded polyester which is treated with a protective coating to stabilize the fibers and to reduce "bearding," a process in which batting fibers work their way out through the quilt fabrics; and wool and silk battings, which are generally more expensive and usually only dry-cleanable.

Whichever batting you choose, read the manufacturer's instructions closely for any special notes on care or preparation. When you're ready to use your chosen batting in a project, cut batting the same size as the prepared backing.

ASSEMBLING THE QUILT
1. Examine wrong side of quilt top closely; trim any seam allowances and clip any threads that may show through the front of the quilt. Press quilt top.
2. If quilt top is to be marked before layering, mark quilting lines (see **Marking Quilting Lines**, page 117).
3. Place backing wrong side up on a flat surface. Use masking tape to tape edges of backing to surface. Place batting on top of backing fabric. Smooth batting gently, being careful not to stretch or tear. Center quilt top right side up on batting.

4. When machine quilting, use 1" rustproof safety pins to "pin-baste" all layers together, spacing pins approximately 4" apart. Begin at the center and work toward the outer edges to secure all layers. If possible, place pins away from areas that will be quilted, although pins may be removed as needed when quilting.

MACHINE QUILTING METHODS

Use the same color general-purpose thread in the needle and bobbin to avoid "dots" of bobbin thread being pulled to the surface and to add pattern and dimension without adding contrasting color. Use general-purpose thread in the bobbin and decorative thread for stitching, such as metallic, variegated or contrasting-colored general-purpose thread, when you desire the quilting to be more pronounced.

Straight-Line Machine Quilting

The term "straight-line" is somewhat deceptive, since curves (especially gentle ones) as well as straight lines can be stitched with this technique.

1. Set the stitch length for 6 – 10 stitches per inch and attach the walking foot to sewing machine.
2. After pin-basting, decide which section of the quilt will have the longest continuous quilting line, oftentimes the area from center top to center bottom. Leaving the area exposed where you will place your first line of quilting, roll up each edge of the quilt to help reduce the bulk, keeping fabrics smooth. Smaller projects may not need to be rolled.
3. Start stitching at beginning of longest quilting line, using very short stitches for the first 1/4" to "lock" beginning of quilting line. Stitch across project, using one hand on each side of the walking foot to slightly spread the fabric and to guide the fabric through the machine. Lock stitches at end of quilting line.
4. Continue machine quilting, stitching longer quilting lines first to stabilize the quilt before moving on to other areas.

Free-Motion Machine Quilting

Free-motion quilting may be free form or may follow a marked quilting pattern.

1. Use a darning foot and drop or cover feed dogs. Pull up bobbin thread and hold both thread ends while you stitch 2 or 3 stitches in place to lock thread. Cut threads near quilt surface.
2. Place hands lightly on quilt on either side of darning foot to slightly spread fabric and to move fabric through the machine. Even stitch length is achieved by using smooth, flowing hand motion and steady machine speed. Slow machine speed and fast hand movement will create long stitches. Fast machine speed and slow hand movement will create short stitches. Move quilt sideways, back and forth, in a circular motion, or in a random motion to create the desired designs; do not rotate quilt. Lock stitches at the end of each quilting line.

MAKING A HANGING SLEEVE

Attaching a hanging sleeve to the back of your wall hanging or quilt before the binding is added allows you to display your completed project on a wall.

1. Measure width of quilt top edge and subtract 1". Cut piece of fabric 7" wide by the determined measurement.
2. Press short edges of fabric piece 1/4" to wrong side; press edges 1/4" to wrong side again and machine stitch in place.
3. Matching wrong sides, fold piece in half lengthwise to form a tube.
4. Match raw edges and stitch hanging sleeve to center top edge on back of wall hanging.
5. Bind wall hanging, treating the hanging sleeve as part of the backing.
6. Blind stitch bottom of hanging sleeve to backing, taking care not to stitch through to front of quilt.

BINDING

Binding encloses the raw edges of your quilt. Because of its stretchiness, bias binding works well for binding projects with curves or rounded corners and tends to lie smooth and flat in any given circumstance. Binding may also be cut from the straight lengthwise or crosswise grain of fabric.

MAKING CONTINUOUS BIAS BINDING

Bias strips for binding can simply be cut and pieced to the desired length. However, when a long length of binding is needed, the "continuous" method is quick and accurate.

1. Cut a square from binding fabric the size indicated in the project instructions. Cut square in half diagonally to make 2 triangles.
2. With right sides together and using a $1/4$" seam allowance, sew triangles together (**Fig. 15**); press seam allowance open.

Fig. 15

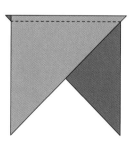

3. On wrong side of fabric, draw lines $2^1/4$" apart (**Fig. 16**). Cut off any remaining fabric less than this width.

Fig. 16

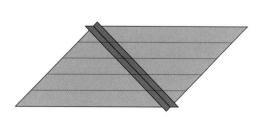

4. With right sides inside, bring short edges together to form a tube; match raw edges so that first drawn line of top section meets second drawn line of bottom section (**Fig. 17**).

Fig. 17

5. Carefully pin edges together by inserting pins through drawn lines at the point where drawn lines intersect, making sure the pins go through intersections on both sides. Using a $1/4$" seam allowance, sew edges together. Press seam allowance open.
6. To cut continuous strip, begin cutting along first drawn line (**Fig. 18**). Continue cutting along drawn line around tube.

Fig. 18

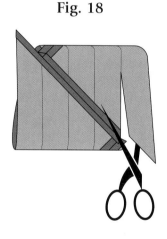

7. Trim ends of bias strip square.
8. Matching wrong sides and raw edges, press bias strip in half lengthwise to complete binding.

MAKING STRAIGHT-GRAIN BINDING

1. Sew binding strips together end-to-end with a diagonal seam (**Fig. 19**) to achieve determined length.

Fig. 19

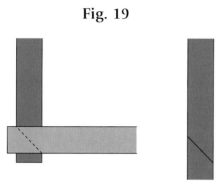

2. Matching wrong sides and raw edges, press strip in half lengthwise to complete binding.

PAT'S MACHINE-SEWN BINDING

For a quick and easy finish when attaching straight-grain binding with overlapped corners, Pat sews her binding to the back of the quilt and Machine Blanket Stitches it in place on the front, eliminating all hand stitching. You can Machine Straight Stitch or hand Blindstitch the binding to the front of the quilt instead of Machine Blanket Stitching.

1. Using a narrow zigzag, stitch around quilt close to the raw edges (**Fig. 20**). Trim backing and batting even with edges of quilt top.

Fig. 20

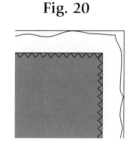

2. Matching raw edges and using a $1/4$" seam allowance, sew a length of binding to top and bottom edges on wrong side of quilt.

3. Fold binding over to quilt front and pin pressed edges in place, covering stitching line (**Fig. 21**); Blanket Stitch, Straight Stitch, or Blindstitch binding close to pressed edge. Trim ends of top and bottom binding even with edges of quilt top.

Fig. 21

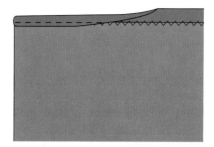

4. Leaving approximately $1^1/2$" of binding at each end, stitch a length of binding to wrong side of each side of quilt.

5. Trim each end of binding $1/2$" longer than bound edge. Fold under each raw end of binding (**Fig. 22**); pin in place. Fold binding over to quilt front and Blanket Stitch, Straight Stitch, or Blindstitch in place, as in Step 3.

Fig. 22

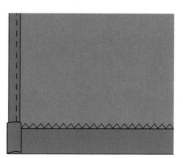

ATTACHING BINDING WITH MITERED CORNERS

1. Beginning with one end near center on bottom edge of quilt, lay binding around quilt to make sure that seams in binding will not end up at a corner. Adjust placement if necessary. Matching raw edges of binding to raw edge of quilt top, pin binding to right side of quilt along one edge.

2. When you reach the first corner, mark ¼" from corner of quilt top (**Fig. 23**).

Fig. 23

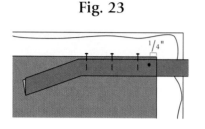

3. Beginning approximately 10" from end of binding and using a ¼" seam allowance, sew binding to quilt, backstitching at beginning of stitching and at mark (**Fig. 24**). Lift needle out of fabric and clip thread.

Fig. 24

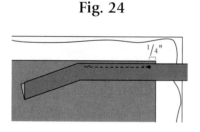

4. Fold binding as shown in **Figs. 25** and **26** and pin binding to adjacent side, matching raw edges. When you reach the next corner, mark ¼" from edge of quilt top.

Fig. 25

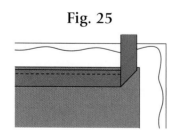

Fig. 26

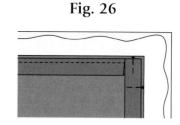

5. Backstitching at edge of quilt top, sew pinned binding to quilt (**Fig. 27**); backstitch when you reach the next mark. Lift needle out of fabric and clip thread.

Fig. 27

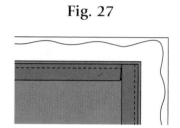

6. Continue sewing binding to quilt, stopping approximately 10" from starting point (**Fig. 28**).

Fig. 28

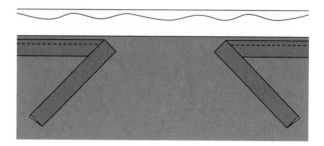

7. Bring beginning and end of binding to center of opening and fold each end back, leaving a ¼" space between folds (**Fig. 29**). Finger-press folds.

Fig. 29

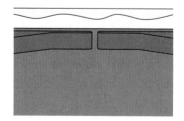

8. Unfold ends of binding and draw a line across wrong side in finger-pressed crease. Draw a line through the lengthwise pressed fold of binding at same spot to create a cross mark. With edge of ruler at marked cross, line up 45° angle marking on ruler with one long side of binding. Draw a diagonal line from edge to edge. Repeat on remaining end, making sure that the two lines are angled the same way (**Fig. 30**).

Fig. 30

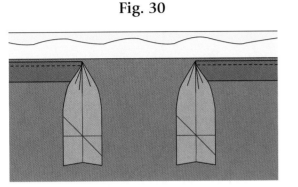

9. Matching right sides and diagonal lines, pin binding ends together at right angles (**Fig. 31**).

Fig. 31

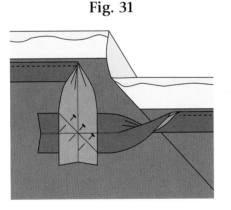

10. Machine stitch along diagonal line, removing pins as you stitch (**Fig. 32**).

Fig. 32

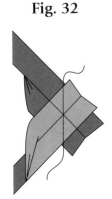

11. Lay binding against quilt to double-check that it is correct length.
12. Trim binding ends, leaving $1/4$" seam allowance; press seam open. Stitch binding to quilt.
13. Trim backing and batting a scant $1/4$" larger than quilt top so that batting and backing will fill the binding when it is folded over to quilt backing.
14. On one edge of quilt, fold binding over to quilt backing and pin pressed edge in place, covering stitching line (**Fig. 33**). On adjacent side, fold binding over, forming a mitered corner (**Fig. 34**). Repeat to pin remainder of binding in place.

Fig. 33

Fig. 34

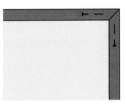

15. Blindstitch, page 125, (**Fig.39**) binding to backing, taking care not to stitch through to front of quilt.

SIGNING AND DATING YOUR QUILT

A completed quilt is a work of art and should be signed and dated. There are many different ways to do this and numerous books on the subject. The label should reflect the style of the quilt, the occasion or person for which it was made, and the quilter's own particular talents. Following are suggestions for recording the history of quilt or adding a sentiment for future generations.

- Embroider the quilter's name, the date, and any additional information on the quilt top or backing. Using low contrasting floss, such as cream floss on a white label, will leave a subtle record. Using bright or contrasting floss will make the information stand out.

- Make a label from muslin and use a permanent fabric marker to write the information. Use different colored permanent markers to make the label more decorative. Stitch the label to the back of the quilt.

- Use photo-transfer paper to add an image to a white or cream fabric label. Stitch the label to the back of the quilt.

- Piece an extra block from the quilt top to use as a label. Add the information with a permanent fabric pen. Appliqué the block to the back of the quilt.

- Write a message on an appliquéd design from the quilt top. Stitch the appliqué to the back of the quilt.

HAND STITCHES

Back Stitch

Come up at 1, go down at 2, and come up at 3 (**Fig. 35**). Continue working as shown in **Fig. 36**. Length of stitches may be varied as desired.

Fig. 35

Fig. 36

Blanket Stitch

Come up at 1, go down at 2, and come up at 3, keeping thread below point of needle (**Fig. 37**). Continue working as shown in **Fig. 38**.

Fig. 37

Fig. 38

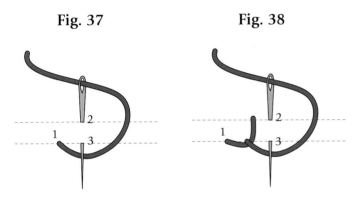

Couching Stitch

Come up at 1, go down at 2. Continue until vine is evenly covered by stitches (**Fig. 40**).

Fig. 40

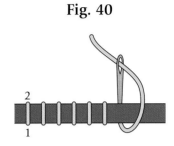

Cross Stitch

Come up at 1 and go down at 2. Come up at 3 and go down at 4 (**Fig. 41**).

Fig. 41

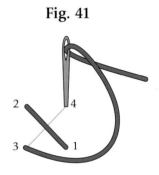

Blind Stitch

Come up at 1, go down at 2, and come up at 3 (**Fig. 39**). Length of stitches may be varied as desired.

Fig. 39

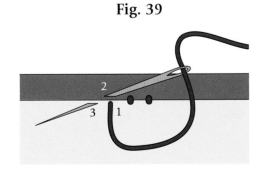

French Knot

Follow **Figs. 42 – 45** to complete French Knots. Come up at 1. Wrap thread once around needle and insert needle at 2, holding end of thread with non-stitching fingers. Tighten knot, then pull needle through, holding floss until it must be released.

Fig. 42   **Fig. 43**

Fig. 44   **Fig. 45**

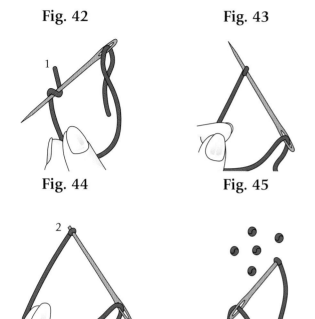

Running Stitch

The running stitch consists of a series of straight stitches with the stitch length equal to the space between stitches. Come up at 1, go down at 2. (**Fig. 46**).

Fig. 46

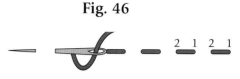

Stem Stitch

Come up at 1. Keeping thread below the stitching line, go down at 2 and come up at 3. Go down at 4 and come up at 5 (**Fig. 47**).

Fig. 47

Straight Stitch

Come up at 1 and go down at 2 (**Fig. 48**). Length of stitches may be varied as desired.

Fig. 48

Metric Conversion Chart

Inches x 2.54 = centimeters (cm)	Yards x .9144 = meters (m)
Inches x 25.4 = millimeters (mm)	Yards x 91.44 = centimeters (cm)
Inches x .0254 = meters (m)	Centimeters x .3937 = inches (")
	Meters x 1.0936 = yards (yd)

Standard Equivalents

1/8"	3.2 mm	0.32 cm	1/8 yard	11.43 cm	0.11 m
1/4"	6.35 mm	0.635 cm	1/4 yard	22.86 cm	0.23 m
3/8"	9.5 mm	0.95 cm	3/8 yard	34.29 cm	0.34 m
1/2"	12.7 mm	1.27 cm	1/2 yard	45.72 cm	0.46 m
5/8"	15.9 mm	1.59 cm	5/8 yard	57.15 cm	0.57 m
3/4"	19.1 mm	1.91 cm	3/4 yard	68.58 cm	0.69 m
7/8"	22.2 mm	2.22 cm	7/8 yard	80 cm	0.8 m
1"	25.4 mm	2.54 cm	1 yard	91.44 cm	0.91 m

EDITORIAL STAFF

Vice President and Editor-in-Chief: Sandra Graham Case. Executive Director of Publications: Cheryl Nodine Gunnells. Senior Director of Publications: Susan White Sullivan. Director of Designer Relations: Debra Nettles. Director of Special Projects: Susan Wiles. Director of Quilt Publications: Cheryl Johnson. Senior Director of Prepress: Mark Hawkins. Director of Art Publications: Rhonda Hodge Shelby. Technical Editor: Lisa Lancaster. Technical Writer: Jean Lewis. Editorial Writer: Susan McManus Johnson. Lead Graphic Artist: Lora Puls. Graphic Artists: Dayle Carozza and Frances Huddleston. Imaging Technician: Mark R. Potter. Photography Coordinator: Katherine Atchison. Contributing Photographer: Ken West. Contributing Photography Stylist: Jan Nobles. Publishing Systems Administrator: Becky Riddle. Publishing Systems Assistants: Clint Hanson, Josh Hyatt, and John Rose.

BUSINESS STAFF

Chief Operating Officer: Tom Siebenmorgen. Vice President, Sales and Marketing: Pam Stebbins. Director of Sales and Services: Margaret Reinold. Vice President, Operations: Jim Dittrich. Comptroller, Operations: Rob Thieme. Retail Customer Service Managers: Stan Raynor. Print Production Manager: Fred F. Pruss.

We have made every effort to ensure that these instructions are accurate and complete. We cannot, however, be responsible for human error, typographical mistakes, or variations in individual work.

ISBN 1-60140-121-3

10 9 8 7 6 5 4 3 2 1

Look for these other Leisure Arts publications by Pat Sloan

Learn to Applique with Pat Sloan
Leaflet #3784

Pat Sloan's
I Can't Believe I'm Quilting
Leaflet #3649

Learn to Bead with Pat Sloan
Leaflet #4389

The Best of Pat Sloan Applique
Leaflet #3799

Crooked Cabin Quilts
Leaflet #3874

Bugs, Blooms & Bullfrogs
Leaflet #3900

Friend-to-Freind Quilts & More
Leaflet #3681

Quilt the Seasons with
Pat Sloan
Leaflet #3574

Folksy Favorites
Leaflet #3391